Canapes, Hors d'oeuvres, other Snacks

APPETIZERS were once savory trifles to be served with cocktails or sherry before dinner. In recent years they have gained new importance. Influenced by the French hors d'oeuvres, the Swedish smörgasbord, the Russian zakuska, the Italian antipasto or the Greek oretika, they are now more varied, more elaborate, and some of them are hearty enough to appear as the principal fare for a special luncheon or a late evening buffet. In any language they must always spell the same charm—be alluring to the eye and the stomach. They must make you want to eat more and more. To the French hors d'oeuvres is a general term for appetizers but Americans tend to apply the term to any "taste-teasing" bit of food that can be eaten with the fingers. If it is hot or has a sauce or marinade, it will be speared on a cocktail pick, but it is usually tiny enough not to require a fork. Canapés are simply hors d'oeuvres served on a bread or other edible base. Toast cut in fancy shapes, cocktail puffs, crêpes, tiny biscuits, timbale cases, crackers and potato chips serve the same purpose as the tiny shapes of bread. Canapés along with piquant bits of food on picks, peanuts, cheese popcorn, olives, crisp vegetables and the like are standbys for cocktail parties.

When the occasion calls for it, they may be extremely elaborate, varied, attractively garnished. The extreme example would be the Swedish smörgasbord—the beautifully appointed table laden with countless varieties of food. Many of them are far too heavy to be classified as appetizers. In fact restaurants in this country which offer Swedish food often list the smörgasbord as a meal in itself. Foods on a typical smörgasbord will include several varieties of bread, imported and domestic cheeses, all sorts of cold cuts of meat, three or four varieties of herring, several sweet and sour dishes, tiny meat balls, spaghetti, egg dishes, anchovies, caviar, crisp vegetables, shrimp and other seafood, and even a variety of salads.

Russian appetizers (zakuska) are served in almost as great a variety and are highly flavored. Caviar, salted herring, salted mushrooms, cucumbers, pickled beets and salmon are the most popular. Vegetables are prominent among the Italian antipasto and selections are very similar in the Greek oretika. Among those offered you will find green pickled peppers, pimiento halves, sliced beets, tomatoes, cucumber,

3

pickled mushrooms, pickled cauliflower and celery hearts along with cheeses, and sliced salami or other meats.

The recipes that follow are extremely varied and give specific methods and seasonings. Nevertheless these recipes should in the last analysis serve only as a guide. They are presented with the suggestion that each be sampled and seasoned to taste as they are made. We believe they will stimulate your imagination and that you will want to elaborate on them and evolve your own favorites. With these hundreds of recipes as a base, you can evolve many thousands of variations with contrasts in colors, textures, designs, and seasonings. They include so many favorite flavors and foods that when the impromptu occasion arises anyone can find enough ingredients on the pantry shelf to make up a delectable array of dainties.

Canape Bases and Butters

TOASTED CANAPE BASES

Cut rounds, squares or fancy shapes from thin bread slices with cooky or sandwich cutters. Place on broiler rack in preheated broiler oven. Place rack about 3 inches from flame. Toast bread on one side. Brush toasted side with melted butter or margarine. Spread appetizer mixture on untoasted side. Savory butters add flavor to canapé bases and many of them may be used, if applied liberally, without any additional canapé spread. A wide variety is given in this book.

HOW TO MAKE APPETIZERS

Abe "Dobby" Dobkin

Consulting Editor

of World Wide Liquors, Inc.; President, Illinois Liquor Store Association, Board Member, National Liquor Store Association; Past Chairman, La Bonne Vie Wine and Food Society; Member, Chaine Des Rotisseurs; Member, Compagnon de Bordeaux.

Countryside Books

CONTENTS

Cover photo courtesy of The National Hot Dog and Sausage Council.

1976 REVISED EDITION

A. B. Morse Co.
200 James St., Barrington, Ill. 60010

SAUTEED BREAD BASES #1

Cut bread into desired shapes. Sauté on one side in a little butter or margarine in a heavy skillet over very low heat. Drain on absorbent paper. Spread plain side with desired canapé spreads.

SAUTEED BREAD BASES #2

Cut bread into desired shapes. Toast on one side as in Toasted Canapé Bases. Sauté untoasted side as in Sautéed Bread Bases #1. Drain. Spread untoasted side.

Note: You'll find that sautéed canapé bases are more desirable than ordinary toasted bread bases. They have far more flavor. All canapé bases should be spread as close to serving time as possible. Allowing them to stand too long will ruin them. If possible don't spread them more than ½ hour before serving time.

VARIETY CRACKER BASES

Use crisp savory crackers. Just brush with melted butter and delicately brown in a moderate oven (350° F.). For variations, sprinkle before toasting with caraway seed, celery salt, garlic salt, grated cheese or paprika.

SAVORY CRISP BREAD STICKS

Trim crusts from bread slices. Cut slices into strips. Brush with melted butter or margarine. Roll half the strips in grated Parmesan cheese and the balance in celery seed. Toast in moderate oven (350° F.) about 15 minutes.

MELBA TOAST

Cut stale bread into ¼-inch slices. Bake in slow oven (300° F.) until brown and dry (15 to 20 minutes).

TOAST STRIPS

Cut bread slices ⅓ inch thick. Remove crusts. Spread butter on both sides. Cut slices into ½-inch strips. Lightly brown under broiler.

PUFFY CRACKER BASES

Soak tiny soda crackers in ice water for 8 minutes. Drain on absorbent paper and remove to greased cooky sheet with a spatula. Brush with melted butter. Bake in very hot oven (450° F.) for 10 minutes. Reduce heat to moderate (350° F.) and allow to dry out for about 20 minutes. They should be crisp and delicately browned.

These cracker bases may be varied by sprinkling with grated cheese, caraway seed or finely chopped nuts before baking, or by mixing into the melted butter a little curry powder and paprika.

Many of the recipes in this book call for puff paste, plain pastry, or baking powder biscuits. The basic recipes offered here have been adjusted in size to conform to recipes such as Liver Sausage Turnovers, Sardine Surprises, Waffled Wafers, etc., which require pastry and biscuit mixes. For those special occasions when you really want to put forth some extraordinary effort, you'll find that tiny patty shells and other puff paste shapes filled with your favorite canapé spreads are ideal.

PLAIN PASTRY

1 cup all-purpose flour   ½ cup shortening
½ teaspoon salt   Cold water

Mix and sift flour and salt. Cut in shortening with a pastry blender or two knives until mixture resembles small peas. Add cold water in small amounts, stirring lightly with a fork and tossing pieces of dough aside as soon as formed. Use only enough water to make particles hold together. Wrap dough in waxed paper and chill 10 to 15 minutes. Roll pastry out on a lightly floured board to ⅛ inch thickness and use in recipes calling for plain pastry. Baking times and temperatures are given in each recipe. The usual temperature for plain pastry is 450° F. and the time for most hors d'oeuvres baked in plain pastry is 15 to 20 minutes.

CHEESE STICKS

Prepare Plain Pastry. Roll out ⅛ inch thick. Sprinkle heavily with grated cheese and paprika, if desired. Fold in half, sprinkle again and roll out. Repeat twice. Cut into strips 3 to 4 inches long and ½ inch wide. Chill. Bake in very hot oven (450° F.) about 8 minutes.

PASTRY CANAPE BASES

Prepare Plain Pastry. Roll out ⅛ inch thick and cut into fancy shapes. Bake in very hot oven (450° F.) about 15 minutes. For variety, sprinkle before baking with allspice, cardamon, caraway, celery seed, coriander, curry powder, mace, mustard, paprika or grated cheese. Use with desired canapé spreads.

BAKING POWDER BISCUITS

2 cups sifted all-purpose flour
3 teaspoons baking powder
½ to 1 teaspoon salt

4 tablespoons shortening
⅔ to ¾ cup milk

Mix and sift flour, baking powder and salt. Cut or rub in shortening.
Add milk to make a soft dough. Place on a floured board and knead
lightly for not more than 30 seconds, using as little flour on board
as possible. Roll out to ½ inch thickness and cut with biscuit cutters
to make biscuits or use recipe for hot hors d'oeuvres as indicated in
recipes such as Waffled Wafers, Quickie Meat Rolls, Quick Franks
In Blanket, etc. For a more highly seasoned biscuit mix increase salt
to 1 teaspoon. This recipe makes fourteen 2-inch biscuits. Bake
biscuits in very hot oven (450° F.) 10 to 15 minutes, depending on
the thickness or until they are golden brown. Serve immediately.

PUFF PASTE

1 cup butter
2 cups sifted all-purpose flour
¼ teaspoon salt

6 tablespoons ice cold water
(about)

Wash butter by placing it in a mixing bowl, holding it under cold
running water and squeezing and pressing with hands until it is
pliable and waxy. Reserve ¼ cup butter; form balance into a square
and chill thoroughly before using. Mix and sift flour and salt twice;
cut in the butter with pastry blender or two knives. Mix to a light
dough with the water, adding a little at a time and only enough to
moisten thoroughly. Form into a compact ball without overworking
and set aside 20 minutes. Roll out on a lightly floured board into a
rectangular shape about ¼ inch thick. Place washed chilled butter in
center of lower half of sheet. Fold upper half over butter. Press edges
firmly together. Roll out again until about ¼ inch thick. Fold together from opposite sides like a sheet to be fitted into an envelope.
Again press the edges together. Wrap in waxed paper and chill about
25 minutes but not in contact with ice. Place on board again; repeat
rolling and folding process altogether four times, chilling the last
time for about an hour. Each rolling should be done in an opposite
direction from the last so that the butter is combined and spread
evenly. The dough may be wrapped in waxed paper and kept in the
refrigerator for several days.

To bake Puff Paste: Shape and chill thoroughly. Arrange on baking
sheets covered with 2 thicknesses of heavy brown paper. Bake in extremely hot oven (500° F.) and reduce heat 50° every 5 minutes
down to moderate (350° F.). Turn as needed to brown evenly. Some

pastry cooks like to bake puff paste at a uniform heat of 500° F. but in this case the paste must be covered with heavy waxed paper after 10 minutes baking.

Patty Shells: Roll puff paste ¼ inch thick. Cut into 3-inch rounds with floured cutter. Cut out centers from half of rounds with a smaller cutter. Moisten underside of each ring with cold water. Place 1 on each full round. Press down lightly. Bake smaller rounds to use as covers. Bake as directed for Puff Paste.

Bouchées: Follow method for Patty Shells, rolling pastry ⅛ inch thick and making cases smaller.

Vol-au-Vent: Work with about ¼ of pastry, keeping remainder chilled until needed. Roll paste ⅓ inch thick. Cut an oval with floured mold or knife. Brush outer edge with water. Add a rim of pastry about ¾ inch wide. Prick several places with fork, chill and bake. If desired, bake smaller ovals for covers, using the paste from center of outer rims. Watch carefully and cover with paper if it browns too quickly.

COCKTAIL CREPES

½ cup sifted all-purpose flour   2 egg yolks, beaten
½ teaspoon salt   1 cup water

Mix and sift flour and salt. Mix egg yolks and water. Combine the two mixtures and beat until smooth. Bake on a greased griddle or skillet. Cool and spread with desired canapé filling and roll. Yield: about 20.

TINY TIMBALE CASES

Very small timbale cases make attractive hors d'oeuvres when filled with anchovy paste, caviar, cream cheese or other desired spreads.

1 cup sifted all-purpose flour   ⅔ cup milk
½ teaspoon salt   1 egg, well beaten
½ teaspoon sugar   1 tablespoon melted shortening

Mix and sift dry ingredients. Stir in milk and beaten egg. Add shortening and beat well. Place some of the batter in a cup. Dip the timbale iron on the end of its handle into deep fat. Heat the fat to 375° F. Drain out iron and dip into batter in cup. Allow batter to coat iron only ¾ of the way to top. Dip in hot fat and fry 1 to 2 minutes, or until golden brown. Remove from hot iron at once. Drain on absorbent paper. Fill as desired.

Cocktail Puff Shells

CANAPE PUFFS

½ cup water
¼ cup butter
⅛ teaspoon salt

½ cup sifted all-purpose flour
2 eggs

Place water, butter and salt in saucepan. Bring to brisk boil. Reduce heat and add flour all at once, stirring vigorously with a wooden spoon until mixture is thick and glossy. Remove from heat. Add eggs, one at a time, beating thoroughly after each addition. Continue beating until dough is thick and smooth and breaks off when spoon is raised. Spoon onto greased baking sheet in ¾-inch rounds, placing shapes 1½ inches apart. Bake in hot oven (400° F.) 15 minutes. (If preferred, dough may be stored in refrigerator several hours or overnight.) When cool, cut slit in side and fill with fillings such as fish flakes, sour cream, cheese and olive, etc. Chill in refrigerator until ready to serve. Yield: 2½ dozen.

Fried Puff Shells (Queen Fritters): Prepare the puff shell mixture above. Scrape mixture from tablespoon into deep hot fat (375° F.). Use 1 rounded tablespoon per puff. Fry until a nice crust has formed, turning frequently (about 12 minutes). Drain and cut off tops of shells. Fill with desired filling and replace tops. Yield: 6 large shells.

CHEESE FILLED PUFFS

Prepare the recipe for Canapé Puffs. When baked, cut a slit at sides and insert ½-inch cubes of sharp American cheese which have been sprinkled with cayenne. Put 1 cube in each puff. At serving time, reheat in a hot oven (400° F.) about 5 minutes.

SIMPLE CHEESE PUFFS

¼ pound grated American cheese
¼ cup butter

½ cup sifted all-purpose flour
Dash of cayenne

Blend cheese and butter thoroughly. Work in the flour and cayenne. Chill 2 hours or longer. Roll into balls 1 inch in diameter. Bake in very hot oven (450° F.) 15 minutes. Yield: 30 puffs.

ANCHOVY STICKS OR RINGS

1 cup sifted all-purpose flour
⅓ cup butter

2 tablespoons anchovy paste
Cold water

Cut the butter into the flour with a pastry blender or two knives. Rub in the anchovy paste and add enough water to make a dough that will roll. Cut into sticks and bake in a very hot oven (450° F.) about 5 minutes. To form rings, fasten the ends of the sticks together or cut with a ring cutter, then bake.

CANAPE PIES

Canapé pies are popular for impromptu gatherings because they can be prepared quickly from supplies on the pantry shelf. To prepare a pie, cut a thin slice the length of a loaf of bread. For a special flavor use a round loaf of rye or pumpernickel. Spread the slice with a soft butter. Then starting in the center spread with separate rings of seasoned canapé spreads. Use spreads that contrast in colors and blend well in flavors. Separate each spread with rings of seasoned cream cheese. Apply the cream cheese with a pastry tube to give a nice decorative effect. Serve the pie, cut into small wedges, around a pile of olives. Specific, colorful examples follow.

RAINBOW CANAPE WHEEL

Cut thin slices of pumpernickel or steamed brown bread. Spread with softened butter. Place a slice of hard-cooked egg in the center. Spread red caviar around the egg slice in a narrow strip. Soften cream cheese with mayonnaise and color half of it green with vegetable coloring. Spread around caviar. Add a circle of black caviar, then a circle of white cream cheese. Edge with red caviar. Chill and serve cut into pie-shaped wedges.

10

PEGGY'S CANAPE PIE

Cut a large round loaf of rye bread in circular slices ¼ inch thick. Spread with soft butter. Place a teaspoon of caviar in the center. Surround with a ring of cream cheese, then with a ring of rolled anchovies, a ring of chopped ripe olives and another ring of cream cheese. Garnish the outer edge with halves of cooked or canned shrimp, whole stuffed green olives, and small pickled onions, alternating the foods. Chill and serve in pie-shaped wedges.

COCKTAIL "CAKE"

The cocktail "cake" may be made from a commercial bakery loaf if you use one of the small round loaves of white, rye or pumpernickel made by Swedish, Jewish, German, French or Italian bakeries. You may prefer, however, to bake your own loaf in a deep round pan using a prepared mix or half of a roll recipe. After baking, cool and remove crusts with a very sharp knife. Cut the loaf into 4 slices to form 4 "layers" of the cocktail "cake." Spread the individual layers with sticky sandwich fillings. For example, chicken salad alternating with vegetable salad, egg salad alternating with fish salad. Put the spread slices together to form original shape of loaf. Frost the loaf with softened cream cheese. Garnish as desired with sliced olives, pickles, radishes, etc. Chill thoroughly in refrigerator. To serve, place on a large round platter and surround with vegetable hors d'oeuvres. Cut into individual wedges as you would a cake.

CANAPE BUTTERS

Savory butters add flavor to canapés. If desired, some may be used alone without additional spreads. To prepare any of the following savory butters, mix the ingredients into ¼ cup of creamed butter. They keep well in the refrigerator if stored in a covered container. Larger quantities may be made by increasing the ingredients proportionately. If the butter is hard when you want to use it, cream it enough to soften, before spreading on canapés.

Anchovy Butter: Use 1 tablespoon anchovy paste or mashed anchovy fillets and ½ teaspoon lemon juice.

Caper Butter: Use 1 tablespoon finely minced capers.

Caviar Butter: Use 2 teaspoons caviar, ¼ teaspoon grated onion, and a few drops of lemon juice.

Cheese Butter: Use ¼ cup soft snappy cheese.

Chili Butter: Use 2 tablespoons chili sauce.

11

Chive Butter: Use 1 tablespoon finely minced chives and 1 teaspoon lemon juice.

Chutney Butter: Use 1 tablespoon chutney.

Crabmeat Butter: Use 3 tablespoons finely shredded crabmeat and ½ teaspoon lemon juice.

Curry Butter: Use ¼ teaspoon curry powder.

Egg Butter: Use 2 mashed hard-cooked eggs, ½ teaspoon lemon juice, a dash of Tabasco sauce, and salt and pepper to taste.

Garlic Butter: Use 1 small clove garlic, minced very fine.

Green Pepper Butter: Use 2 tablespoons grated green pepper, well-drained, and a few drops of lemon juice.

Green Savory Butter: Use 3 tablespoons spinach purée, 1 tablespoon anchovy paste, a dash of paprika, 1 teaspoon chopped capers, and salt to taste.

Herring Butter: Use 2 teaspoons ground smoked herring or herring paste, and a few drops of lemon juice.

Honey Butter: Use ¼ cup honey.

Horseradish Butter: Use 2 tablespoons drained horseradish.

Ketchup Butter: Use 2 to 3 tablespoons ketchup.

Lemon Butter: Use ½ teaspoon grated lemon rind and 1 tablespoon lemon juice. (Lime or orange rind and juices may be substituted for lemon.)

Liverwurst Butter: Use 2 tablespoons mashed liverwurst sausage and ½ teaspoon grated onion.

Lobster Butter: Use 2 tablespoons lobster paste, ½ teaspoon lemon juice, and a dash each of dry mustard and paprika.

Mint Butter: Use 2 tablespoons minced mint leaves and 1 teaspoon lemon juice.

Mustard Butter: Use 1 tablespoon prepared mustard.

Nut Butter: Use 2 tablespoons finely minced, salted nuts.

Olive Butter: Use ⅛ cup finely chopped green or stuffed olives and a few drops of onion juice.

Olive-Pimiento Butter: Use 1 pimiento, chopped fine, and ⅛ cup finely chopped stuffed olives.

Onion Butter: Use 1 teaspoon onion juice.

Paprika Butter: Use 2 teaspoons paprika and a few drops lemon juice.

Parmesan Butter: Use 2 tablespoons grated Parmesan cheese.

Parsley Butter: Use 2 tablespoons finely minced parsley and a few drops Worcestershire sauce.

Peanut Butter: Use ¼ cup peanut butter, 1 teaspoon honey, and salt to taste.

Pimiento Butter: Use 2 tablespoons mashed pimiento and 1 teaspoon finely chopped drained pickle.

Roquefort Butter: Use 1 tablespoon Roquefort cheese.

Salmon Butter: Use 1 tablespoon salmon paste or mashed smoked salmon (1 ounce) and 1 teaspoon lemon juice.

Sardine Butter: Use 2 tablespoons sardine paste or mashed sardines and ½ teaspoon each lemon juice and onion juice.

Shrimp Butter: Use 2 tablespoons ground cooked or canned shrimp and ¼ teaspoon each lemon juice and onion juice.

Tarragon Butter: Use 2 or 3 tarragon leaves, finely chopped, and a few drops tarragon vinegar.

Watercress Butter: Use 2 tablespoons finely chopped watercress, 1 teaspoon lemon juice, and a few drops Worcestershire sauce.

Worcestershire Sauce Butter: Use ¼ teaspoon Worcestershire sauce.

QUICK MAYONNAISE VARIATIONS

To prepare any of the following dressings, mix the ingredients into 1 cup of mayonnaise. These dressings are called for in various recipes throughout this book.

Green Mayonnaise: Color with green vegetable coloring or spinach purée. For additional variety when used as a dunking bowl, add 1 to 2 teaspoons each of chopped chives, parsley, tarragon, chervil, and dill.

Red Mayonnaise: Tint with red vegetable coloring, or pound a lobster coral, force it through a sieve and add to mayonnaise.

Russian Dressing: Add 1 chopped hard-cooked egg, ¼ cup chili sauce, and 2 tablespoons chopped green pepper.

Horseradish Mayonnaise: Add 3 tablespoons prepared horseradish.

Nippy Mayonnaise: Add 3 teaspoons prepared horseradish, 3 teaspoons prepared mustard, and 1 small chopped sweet pickle.

Savory Mayonnaise: Add ¼ teaspoon each of Worcestershire sauce, paprika, and dry mustard.

Roquefort Mayonnaise: Add 2 tablespoons crumbled Roquefort or blue cheese, a few drops of Worcestershire sauce, 1 tablespoon French dressing, and 1 tablespoon minced chives.

Ravigotte Mayonnaise: Mix and chop ½ cup watercress, ½ cup parsley, 2 teaspoons chives, 1 tablespoon capers, and 4 anchovies. Force mixture through a sieve and add to mayonnaise.

Tartar Sauce: Add 1 tablespoon each of chopped capers, olives, parsley, and pickles. Serve hot or cold.

Dunking Trays, Bowls, Vegetable Hors d'oeuvres

DUNKING trays are among the most popular of drink accompaniments, and they can be relatively simple or very elaborate. Arrange one or two dunking bowls in the center of the tray. Around them place alternate layers of vegetable hors d'oeuvres such as celery, raw carrot cut in strips or very long slices curled in ice water, cauliflower broken and sliced in flowerets, asparagus tips, white and red radishes, green onion, tiny cherry or plum tomatoes, paper-thin slices of turnips, cucumber, and zucchini. You may want to extend the list; however, remember that the vegetables must be washed and iced thoroughly.

You may include cold boiled or hot fried shrimp, tiny fresh or smoked oysters, chunks of lobster or crabmeat. In addition to the suggestions for dunking and spread-your-own bowls that follow you may also want to choose one of the cocktail sauces or a salad dressing like green mayonnaise or Russian dressing. They are especially good with seafood or cubes of avocado. You'll find that a bowl of thick sour cream with chopped chives in it is especially welcome with vegetable hors d'oeuvres.

DUNKING BOWLS

Combine the enumerated ingredients, mix thoroughly and heap into a bowl.

CURRIED CHEESE DUNK

2 cups cottage cheese
6 tablespoons mayonnaise
4 tablespoons cream
3 teaspoons curry powder
1 teaspoon salt

VEGETABLE-CHEESE DUNK

2 cups cottage cheese
¼ cup heavy cream
¼ cup grated raw carrot
½ cup finely cut green onions
¼ cup chopped green pepper
6 radishes, sliced very thin

SOUR CREAM DUNK

2 cups sour cream
1 cup finely chopped green pepper
¼ cup chopped chives
¼ cup chopped parsley
¼ cup thinly sliced radishes
Salt and pepper to taste

PINK MAYONNAISE DUNK

1 cup mayonnaise
½ cup chili sauce or ketchup
Juice of 1 lemon
About 5 drops onion juice

CHIVES-CHEESE DUNK

2 cups cottage cheese
2 tablespoons cream
2 teaspoons horseradish
2 tablespoons chopped chives
1½ teaspoons salt
½ teaspoon pepper

ZIPPY EGG DUNK

4 hard-cooked eggs, minced
3 strips crisp bacon, crumbled
1 teaspoon minced onion
1 teaspoon Worcestershire sauce
1 teaspoon horseradish
Mayonnaise, enough to give nice spreading consistency

15

SARDINE DUNK

8-ounce package cream cheese
2 cans sardine fillets
3 tablespoons minced chives
½ cup minced parsley
Salt
Sweet cream

Soften cream cheese to room temperature. Mash sardines with the oil. Blend cheese, sardines, chives, and parsley. Add salt to taste and enough cream to thin mixture to dunking consistency.

SHRIMP AND COTTAGE CHEESE DUNK

½ pound fresh, cooked shrimp
  or 1 5-ounce can shrimp
1 cup creamed cottage cheese
3 tablespoons chili sauce
½ teaspoon onion juice
½ teaspoon lemon juice
¼ teaspoon Worcestershire
  sauce
About 4 tablespoons milk

Chop cleaned shrimp fine. Combine with cottage cheese, seasonings, and enough milk to make a creamy mixture. Add salt if desired. Pile into bowl.

QUICK SOUR CREAM AND RED CAVIAR DUNK

Combine thick sour cream with red caviar and a few drops of onion juice, to taste. Serve with squares of pumpernickel or rye bread.

CLAM-CREAM CHEESE DUNK

1 garlic clove, cut in half
8-ounce package cream cheese
2 teaspoons lemon juice
1½ teaspoons Worcestershire
  sauce
½ teaspoon salt
Dash of freshly ground pepper
½ cup (7-ounce can) drained
  minced clams
4 tablespoons clam broth

Rub a small mixing bowl with cut garlic clove. Place all remaining ingredients in bowl. Blend well. For a thinner dip, add more broth.

GUACAMOLE (MEXICAN AVOCADO DUNK)

2 soft, ripe avocados, peeled and
  pitted
3 green onions, minced
2 peeled and chopped tomatoes
2 chopped canned chili peppers
  or 1 teaspoon chili powder
Salt and pepper to taste
1 tablespoon lemon juice

Put avocados through a sieve. Mix with onions, tomatoes, and peppers. Add salt and pepper to taste. Add lemon juice. Whip until fluffy.

16

CREAM CHEESE SPREAD-YOUR-OWN BOWLS

In each of the following cream cheese bowls, soften the cream cheese with the cream. Blend thoroughly with the other ingredients and heap into a bowl.

HORSERADISH-CREAM CHEESE BOWL

4 (3-ounce) packages cream cheese
½ cup light cream

3 teaspoons prepared horse-radish
Worcestershire sauce to taste
Minced onion to taste

DEVILED HAM-CREAM CHEESE BOWL

4 (3-ounce) packages cream cheese
½ cup light cream

2 tablespoons deviled ham
1 teaspoon finely chopped chives

AVOCADO-CREAM CHEESE BOWL

3 (3-ounce) packages cream
½ cup light cream
1 large avocado, peeled, pitted and mashed

1½ teaspoons lemon juice
1½ teaspoons onion juice
1 teaspoon salt

Avocado pulp and cream cheese should be about equal in amount.

ROQUEFORT-CREAM CHEESE BOWL

2 (3-ounce) packages cream cheese
½ cup light cream
8 ounces Roquefort or blue cheese

¼ cup finely minced onion
2 teaspoons lemon juice
¾ teaspoon salt

SHRIMP SPREAD-YOUR-OWN BOWL

½ pound cooked, cleaned shrimp
3-ounce package cream cheese
Cream as needed
2 tablespoons prepared horseradish

1 tablespoon chopped parsley
1 teaspoon lemon juice
1 teaspoon Worcestershire sauce
Dash of Tabasco sauce
Salt to taste

Put shrimp through grinder using medium blade. Mash cream cheese with enough cream to moisten thoroughly. Add seasonings and beat until creamy. Beat into shrimp. Heap into bowl. Chill.

17

AVOCADO SPREAD-YOUR-OWN BOWL

1 avocado
1 to 2 teaspoons minced onion
3 tablespoons mayonnaise

Juice of ½ lemon
Salt to taste
3 drops Tabasco sauce

Mash the peeled avocado pulp. Add other ingredients and blend well.

CARLTON CHEESE MOUND

½ pound sharp cheddar cheese
¼ pound Roquefort cheese
3-ounce package cream cheese

Finely chopped chives
Heavy cream
Paprika

Grate cheddar and Roquefort cheese or put through food chopper. Blend with cream cheese, chives, and heavy cream to moisten. Beat until fluffy. Mound on a plate. Sprinkle with paprika.

TOMATO CREAM CHEESE BOWL

1 cut clove garlic
2 very ripe tomatoes
8-ounce package cream cheese

1 teaspoon Worcestershire
sauce
1 teaspoon grated onion
½ teaspoon salt

Rub a chopping bowl with garlic. Chop tomatoes in same bowl until completely mashed. Add remaining ingredients. Beat until smooth. Serve with crackers and potato chips.

ALMOND CHEESE ROLLS

3-ounce package cream cheese
½ pound sharp American
cheese
1 cup unblanched almonds
1 canned pimiento
3 teaspoons lemon juice

1½ teaspoons salt
1 teaspoon Worcestershire sauce
1 teaspoon scraped onion
Dash of cayenne
Paprika
Finely chopped almonds

Put cheese, almonds, and pimiento through food chopper using fine blade. Add lemon juice, salt, Worcestershire sauce, onion, and cayenne. Mix well. Shape into 2 rolls about 7 inches long. Roll 1 in paprika, the other in finely chopped almonds. Wrap in waxed paper. Chill thoroughly. To serve, let guests cut thin slices to place on thin crackers.

CAVIAR SERVICE

When serving caviar by itself, set the jar in a bed of cracked ice. Serve with accompaniments of sour cream, lemon juice, minced onion, and melba toast or dark rye bread. Use both black and red caviar. Imported caviar is expensive, therefore don't hesitate to follow the example of many prominent hostesses by using domestic varieties.

COCKTAIL SAUCES

A bowl of cocktail sauce is almost a necessity in the center of a dunking tray containing seafoods. Many people like a sharp cocktail sauce with vegetable hors d'oeuvres as well.

Standard Cocktail Sauce #1: Mix 1½ cups ketchup, 1 tablespoon horseradish, ¼ cup lemon juice, 1 teaspoon finely chopped celery, 1 tablespoon Worcestershire sauce, a few drops onion juice, a few drops Tabasco sauce, and ½ teaspoon salt. Chill thoroughly. Yield: about 1¾ cups.

Standard Cocktail Sauce # 2: Mix 1 cup ketchup, 4 teaspoons prepared horseradish, ¼ cup lemon juice, 1 teaspoon Worcestershire sauce, a dash of Tabasco sauce, and 1 teaspoon salt. Chill. Yield: about 1½ cups.

Cocktail Dressing: Mix ½ cup mayonnaise 1 tablespoon lemon juice, 1 tablespoon ketchup, 1 tablespoon horseradish, ¼ teaspoon paprika, 3 drops Worcestershire sauce, 2 drops Tabasco sauce, and salt to taste. Chill. Yield: about ¾ cup.

Piquant Cocktail Sauce: Mix ⅓ cup ketchup, 1 teaspoon onion juice, ½ teaspoon Tabasco sauce, and salt and pepper to taste. Chill. Yield: about ⅓ cup.

Celery Cocktail Sauce: Mix ¾ cup ketchup or chili sauce with 2 tablespoons lemon juice, 1 teaspoon Worcestershire sauce, ¼ cup chopped celery, and a dash each of salt and cayenne. Chill. Yield: about 1 cup.

Cucumber Cocktail Sauce: Mix ½ cup chili sauce with 1 teaspoon onion juice, 1 teaspoon lemon juice, ½ cup pared and grated cucumber, and a dash each of pepper, salt, and Tabasco sauce. Chill. Yield: about 1 cup.

Pickle Relish Cocktail Sauce: Mix ¾ cup chili sauce or ketchup with 5 tablespoons sweet pickle relish, 1 teaspoon prepared horseradish, and ½ teaspoon Worcestershire sauce. Chill. Yield: about 1 cup.

19

Vegetable Hors d'Oeuvres with Dip Sauce

VEGETABLE HORS D'OEUVRES

Asparagus Tips: Marinate small tips in French dressing. Sprinkle ends with paprika.

Beets, Plain or Pickled: Use tiny canned beets. They go well with a bowl of sour cream.

Carrot Strips: Wash and scrape young tender carrots. Cut in thin strips lengthwise. Wrap in damp cloth and chill.

Carrot Fans: Wash and scrape young tender carrots. Cut in quarters lengthwise. With a very sharp knife cut each quarter into thin lengthwise slices almost to the end. Spread on ice in a tray. Cover and chill.

Celery Curls: Slit celery on one end about 1½ inches down and at about ⅛-inch intervals. Stalks should be about 3 to 4 inches long. Chill in ice water.

Cauliflowerets: Break cauliflower into small flowerets. Crisp in ice water. Drain and sprinkle with paprika. Or, precook flowerets for just a few minutes, then marinate in sharp French dressing until serving time.

Cucumber Strips: Peel cucumber. Cut in half. Remove seeds. Cut solid part into narrow strips about 3 inches long. Cover with damp cloth. Chill well before serving. Sprinkle with paprika.

Cucumber Slices: Peel cucumber. Score it by running a 4-tined fork down the lengthwise surface of the cucumber. Cut into very thin slices. Chill in a tray of ice. Drain and sprinkle lightly with chopped parsley. When skin is tender, score without peeling and slice, thus adding a touch of color.

Radish Roses: Cut down thin strips of red peel of radishes almost through to stems to form petals. Place radishes in ice water. As they chill the peel will curl back like petals.

Radish Fans: Select firm and rather long radishes. With a very sharp thin knife, cut thin slices crosswise almost through radish. Chill in ice water. The slices spread, fan shaped, as they chill.

Whole Radishes: Select firm red or white radishes. Wash and scrub thoroughly. Cut off stems and root fibers. Wrap in damp cloth. Chill thoroughly in refrigerator.

Scallions: Trim washed green stalks, leaving about 3 inches. Trim onion if skin is loose or shriveled. Chill in ice water.

Marinated Onions: Skin and slice Bermuda onions. Soak in a brine made of 1 cup water to 1 tablespoon salt. Drain and soak in vinegar for 20 to 30 minutes. Drain again. Chill thoroughly.

Stuffed Eggs and Stuffed Celery

Stuffed Eggs and Stuffed Vegetables

STUFFED EGGS

With an endless variety of fillings, stuffed eggs are the most popular of all snacks to serve with cocktails. Hard-cook the eggs in water just below the boiling point for 12 to 15 minutes. If the eggs are taken directly from the refrigerator start them in cold or lukewarm water. Hot water may crack the shells. When done, chill in cold water to prevent darkening of the yolks and to make shelling easier. Cut the eggs in half lengthwise. If you want to, cut them crosswise and trim the bottoms so they won't roll over. Remove the yolks and put through a sieve or mash with a fork. Combine with seasonings and refill the whites of eggs. To give a more decorative effect use a pastry tube. Garnish with chopped parsley, chopped chives, paprika, tiny pearl onions, or slices of stuffed olive. The fillings that follow are for 6 eggs.

DEVILED EGGS

6 *hard-cooked eggs, shelled*
1 *tablespoon cream or
mayonnaise*
1½ *teaspoons vinegar
Dash of pepper*
¾ *teaspoon prepared mustard*
½ *teaspoon Worcestershire
sauce (optional)*
¼ *teaspoon salt*

Remove yolks and mash with a fork. Add seasonings and beat until smooth and fluffy. Refill whites of eggs. Garnish.

Savory Deviled Eggs: Season to taste with additional seasonings such as onion juice, sardines, anchovies, cheese, pickles, olives or chives.

With Caviar: Dip the halves in caviar to cover filling. Sprinkle with a few drops lemon juice.

ANCHOVY STUFFED EGGS

6 *hard-cooked eggs, shelled*
2 *tablespoons anchovy paste*
1 *tablespoon minced chives*
1 *teaspoon lemon juice*

Mash egg yolks with a fork. Blend with other ingredients and refill whites of eggs. Garnish.

CAVIAR STUFFED EGGS #1

6 hard-cooked eggs, shelled
3 tablespoons mayonnaise
2 ounces caviar
¼ teaspoon salt
Pinch of pepper

Mash yolks with a fork. Mix lightly with caviar, mayonnaise, and seasonings. Reserve a little caviar to decorate the top. Refill whites of eggs. Garnish tops with caviar.

CHEESE STUFFED EGGS

6 hard-cooked eggs, shelled
2 tablespoons butter, creamed
⅓ cup grated Swiss cheese
Salt and pepper

Mash yolks with a fork. Blend with butter and cheese. Add seasonings to taste. Refill whites of eggs. Garnish.

CRABMEAT STUFFED EGGS

6 hard-cooked eggs, shelled
½ cup flaked crabmeat
½ cup finely chopped celery
1 tablespoon chopped green pepper
½ teaspoon dry mustard
⅓ cup mayonnaise

Mash yolks with a fork. Combine with other ingredients and refill whites of eggs. Garnish.

DRIED BEEF STUFFED EGGS

6 hard-cooked eggs, shelled
⅓ cup shredded dried beef
Juice of ½ small lemon
¼ teaspoon Worcestershire sauce
2½ tablespoons salad dressing

Frizzle dried beef until slightly crisp in butter in heavy skillet. Mash egg yolks with a fork. Add beef and other ingredients and combine well. Refill whites of eggs. Garnish with paprika or chopped parsley.

HAM STUFFED EGGS

6 hard-cooked eggs, shelled
¼ cup ground ham
1 teaspoon dry mustard
About ½ teaspoon salt
Mayonnaise

Mash yolks with a fork. Blend with other ingredients using enough mayonnaise to form into smooth paste. Refill whites of eggs. Garnish.

23

Deviled Eggs with Scalloped Edges

OTHER STUFFED EGG FILLINGS

1. Chopped celery mixed with mashed egg yolk, moistened with mayonnaise or salad dressing.

2. Crisp bacon mixed with mashed egg yolk and minced parsley, moistened with mayonnaise.

3. Sautéed chicken livers, chopped fine and mixed with mashed egg yolk.

4. Chopped mushrooms and chopped onions sautéed in butter and mixed with mashed egg yolk.

5. Mashed egg yolk mixed with finely chopped pickle, moistened with mayonnaise.

6. Mashed sardines, seasoned with salt and lemon juice, mixed with mashed egg yolk and moistened with mayonnaise.

CAVIAR STUFFED EGGS #2

Quarter hard-cooked eggs. Remove yolks. Fill whites with caviar seasoned with lemon and onion juices. Sprinkle grated yolk on top.

EGG SARDINE HORS D'OEUVRES

Cut hard-cooked eggs in halves, lengthwise. Season with salt, pepper, and paprika. Place a small well-drained sardine or rolled fillet of anchovy over each egg half. Arrange on a crisp lettuce leaf. Garnish with a bit of lemon.

STUFFED VEGETABLES

Pickled Beets: Hollow out tiny pickled beets. Chill and just before serving fill with caviar. Sprinkle lightly with lemon juice and grated onion. Top with a tiny bit of sour cream.

Stuffed Cucumber Slices: Cut cucumber in half crosswise. Pare and remove seeds leaving center hollow. Fill center with Roquefort or seasoned cream cheese spread. Wrap in waxed paper. Chill thoroughly. To serve, cut into ¼-inch slices. Garnish with small green caper.

Stuffed Pickles: Remove centers from dill pickles with a vegetable corer. Fill tightly with a snappy cheese spread, deviled ham, or liver sausage. Chill and cut crosswise into ½-inch slices.

Stuffed Radishes #1: Hollow out radishes with a sharp pointed knife. Crisp in ice water. Stuff with a mixture of caviar, minced parsley, mayonnaise, lemon juice, and onion juice, seasoned to taste.

Stuffed Radishes #2: Prepare radishes as in #1. Fill with an assortment of softened cheeses. In some cases it may be desirable to melt the cheese first and then allow it to cool before stuffing into the shells.

Celery Pinwheels: Cut base from celery bunch. Separate, wash and dry stalks. Fill each stalk with tangy cheese spread. Press stalks together in shape of original bunch and tie with string. Chill. To serve, cut into ¼ to ½-inch slices.

Stuffed Pepper Slices: Select long thin peppers in a variety of shades of green and red. Stuff so that all corners are filled with a seasoned cream cheese mixture. Chill 2 to 3 hours. To serve, cut with a very sharp knife into ¼-inch slices.

Tiny Stuffed Tomatoes: Select firm cherry or plum tomatoes. Cut out centers and stuff with a favorite fish, seafood, or meat mixture.

Tomato-Egg Boats: Cut medium-sized tomatoes in eights and cut out centers, leaving ½-inch thick piece. Chop 2 hard-cooked eggs fine; add ½ teaspoon salt, a little finely chopped celery, 1 tablespoon mayonnaise, and 1 teaspoon mustard-with-horseradish. Fill the tomato boats and garnish with a bit of parsley.

Artichoke Cups: Remove centers from canned artichoke hearts leaving ⅛ inch. Chop centers and add equal quantity of chopped pimiento and ½ quantity chopped browned almonds or peanuts. Fill centers.

Stuffed Brussels Sprouts: Drain cooked or canned Brussels sprouts. Cut out centers and stuff with favorite canapé spread to which may be added the chopped centers of sprouts.

Celery Pinwheels

Stuffed Carrots or Beets: Use new carrots and small beets. Cook until just tender. Remove centers with a vegetable corer and stuff with seasoned cottage cheese. Chill and serve in slices.

STUFFED CELERY

Wash tender celery stalks in cold water to crisp. Trim leaves. Cut large stalks in 2-inch lengths. Fill grooves with any of the following fillings, pressed through pastry tube or spread with knife.

Avocado: Mash avocado pulp. Sprinkle with lemon juice. Season to taste with salt and pepper. Moisten slightly with mayonnaise. Stuff and garnish with bits of pimiento.

Avocado-Flaked Fish: Put soft avocado through a sieve. Mix with flaked fish and chopped stuffed olives. Season with lemon juice. For a sharper flavor, use cayenne pepper or mustard.

Avocado-Roquefort. Mash peeled and pitted avocado. Combine with Roquefort or blue cheese and make a smooth paste, adding lemon juice and onion juice to taste. Stuff and garnish with bits of pimiento.

Cottage Cheese: Season cheese with salt and spread into grooves. Garnish with thin slices of radish with red edge showing.

Cream Cheese: Mix cheese with finely chopped nuts. Spread in celery grooves. Or mix cheese with finely chopped stuffed olives.

Deviled Ham: Combine deviled ham, cream cheese, and mayonnaise to taste. Season with prepared mustard and horseradish.

Egg: Chop hard-cooked eggs fine. Moisten with mayonnaise and season with salt and pepper. Stuff and dust with paprika or minced parsley.

Peanut Butter-Cheese: Blend equal amounts of peanut butter and pimiento cheese.

Roquefort #1: Combine Roquefort style cheese with a little butter or cream cheese. Season with grated onion.

Roquefort #2: Soften 2 ounces Roquefort cheese with 2 tablespoons (1 ounce) butter. Mix in ½ cup crushed pineapple. Spread and sprinkle with paprika.

Sardine: Cut lengths of celery to sardine size. Stuff celery with cream cheese seasoned with onion juice and minced parsley. Lay a small whole sardine on each piece. Garnish with strip of pimiento.

Seafood: Combine tuna fish or other flaked, cooked or canned seafood with a little lemon juice to flavor and mayonnaise to moisten.

STUFFED CELERY TREES

Clean and wash celery thoroughly. Select the well curved stalks and cut them into 2½-inch pieces. Fringe the tops and let stand in ice water. Remove and wipe well. Fill with your favorite celery stuffing. Put pieces together to form a round tree-like stalk and hold them together with a toothpick. When trimmed at the bottom they will stand up, fringe end to the top like a tree.

STUFFED DILL PICKLE SLICES

Remove centers from dill pickles with a vegetable corer. Stuff pickles with a snappy cheese spread, well-seasoned ground cooked meat, mock pâté de foie gras, deviled ham, or liver sausage. Chill thoroughly and cut them crosswise into 1/3-inch slices.

Hors d'oeuvres on Picks

PORCUPINE BALL

Use a large grapefruit, a big red apple, a solid head of cabbage (green or red), or one of the wooden or metal figures made to hold hors d'oeuvres on toothpicks. Any sort of toothpick may be used but the specially made colored cocktail picks are most attractive. On the ends of the picks place stuffed olives, little sweet pickles, rolled anchovy fillets, little cocktail sausages, or other tasty simple hors d'oeuvres or balls on picks. A large variety of suggestions are given in the following pages.

TASTY SIMPLE HORS D'OEUVRES

Anchovy Olives: Select very large olives. Remove pits carefully. Stuff with anchovy paste. Twist a whole anchovy fillet around each. Fasten with picks. Serve with lemon wedges.

Apples and Cheese: Core and cut firm red eating apples into ½-inch slices. Do not pare. Dip in orange juice to prevent darkening. Spread with any sharp cheese. Cut into wedges. Spear each wedge.

Artichoke Hearts #1: Marinate tiny canned artichoke hearts in highly seasoned French dressing to which a clove of garlic has been added. Drain well.

Artichoke Hearts #2: Drain canned artichoke hearts. Wash in salted water. Dry carefully. With a pastry tube pipe edge with cream cheese. Fill center with caviar.

Braunschweiger Olives: Mash Braunschweiger sausage. Form a spoonful at a time into a small patty. Place a small stuffed olive in center and roll into ball to cover olive. Roll the balls in chopped parsley or very finely chopped pecans or walnuts. If nuts are used and they do not stick, add a little butter to sausage when mashing it.

Button Mushrooms: Sauté mushrooms, then chill and marinate in lemon juice. Top each with a slice of stuffed olive.

Cheese Cubes: Marinate tiny cubes of American cheese in chili sauce.

Cheese and Pickled Onion: Place a ½-inch square of American cheese, a tiny slice of pickle, and a tiny pickled onion on each pick.

Frank Quickies: Cut frankfurters in half, lengthwise. Spread the cut surface of half the franks generously with a cheese spread. Top each spread half with an unspread half, pressing back into original shape. Scrape off excess cheese. Wrap in waxed paper. Chill. Cut into ½-inch pieces. Serve on picks.

Frankfurter Ovals: Cut frankfurters on a slant about ½-inch thick. Cover one end with a mixture made of ½ cup cottage cheese seasoned with 2 teaspoons each of mustard-horseradish and minced onion, and 1 teaspoon finely chopped parsley.

Garlic Olives: Rub a small bowl thoroughly with a cut clove of garlic. Put green or ripe olives in bowl. Cover with salad oil. Let stand ½ hour. Drain off oil.

Ham Cubes with Grapes: Spear ham cubes with seedless grapes.

Ham and Pickled Onion: Spear small ham cubes and small pickled onions (or small stuffed olives or cubes of dill or sweet pickle).

Kabob in Variety: Place alternately on pick: sautéed mushroom, tiny pickled onion, olive half, and cheese cube.

Melon and Meat Kabobs: Cut melon into cubes. Dip in lemon juice. Spear each cube with a cube of ham or canned spiced meat.

Olive and Onion Kabobs: Alternate small stuffed olive and small pickled onion on pick.

Oysters: Chill small oysters thoroughly. Marinate in sharp dressing.

Pretzel Stick Dumbbells: Form small balls from tasty cheese. Place a cheese ball at each end of a small pretzel stick.

Prunes: Steam small prunes until tender. Remove pits. Fill with a tangy cheese spread.

Salami: Spear bite-size cubes with small olives.

Sausage Pickups: Cut sausage into cubes. Dip in cream, then roll in finely chopped parsley.

Shrimp with Avocado and Cucumber: Marinate cubes of avocado and pieces of cooked or canned shrimp in French dressing. Spear with cucumber cubes.

Shrimp Curls: Place an ice-cold shrimp in a small leaf of lettuce or romaine. Top with mayonnaise. Roll and secure with a pick.

Shrimp and Pineapple: Spear a small whole shrimp and a cube of canned pineapple on a pick. Provide dunking sauce.

Smoked Salmon, Tongue, or Anchovy Pickles: Wrap thin slices of smoked salmon, cooked tongue, or anchovy fillets around small gherkins. Secure with picks.

Spiced Pineapple Cubes: Sauté pineapple chunks in a little butter or margarine. Sprinkle with brown sugar, spices, and a dash of vinegar. Stir gently until glazed.

Stuffed Cheese Olives: Cut very large stuffed olives in half lengthwise. Cut cheddar cheese into ½-inch squares about ¼ inch deep. Place 1 cheese square between 2 halves of olive and press firmly together.

Stuffed Olives in Anchovy Fillets: Roll each large stuffed olive in an anchovy fillet. Secure with pick.

Swiss and Dill Kabobs: Cut Swiss cheese into ½-inch cubes. Put between 2 thin slices of dill pickle and skewer with pick.

Vienna Sausage-Cheese Cube Kabobs: Spear short pieces of Vienna sausage and cubes of cheddar or Swiss cheese.

NUTMEATS FOR HORS D'OEUVRES

Pecan or Walnut Bonbons: Put perfect pecan or walnut halves together with any cream cheese spread or anchovy paste.

Curried Nutmeats: Toast nutmeats in oven; while toasting sprinkle liberally with curry powder and add a little melted butter or oil.

Garlic Nutmeats: Sprinkle nutmeats with garlic salt and melted butter. Toast in oven until crisp. Or, mash a garlic clove and let stand in butter ½ hour. Strain butter and use to season nutmeats while toasting them.

Zesty Pecans: Add salt and 1 tablespoon melted butter to 1 pound shelled pecans. Mix and toast in slow oven (300° F.) about ½ hour, stirring frequently. After 15 minutes, add 3 tablespoons Worcestershire sauce and a few dashes Tabasco sauce or cayenne pepper.

BALLS ON PICKS

Anchovy Balls: Mash 4 ounces anchovy paste with 2 hard-cooked eggs. Add ¼ cup finely chopped parsley. Season with a few grains cayenne and Worcestershire sauce to taste. Form into tiny balls. Chill thoroughly.

Blackberries: Form small balls of cream cheese. Roll in caviar and press gently into shape to resemble blackberries.

Braunschweiger Balls: Form Braunschweiger sausage into small balls and roll in shredded dried beef.

Burning Bush: Soften 1 package (3 ounces) cream cheese and season with ½ teaspoon minced onion. Form into balls. Roll in minced dried beef.

Camembert Balls: Cut off rind of Camembert cheese. Season cheese with salt and pepper to taste. Soften with butter. Form into tiny balls. Roll in stale rye bread crumbs. Chill thoroughly.

Celery-Cheese Balls: Mix 1 cup finely chopped celery, 1 package (3 ounces) cream cheese, salt and pepper to taste. Roll balls in minced parsley. Chill.

Chipped Beef Balls: Season cream cheese with Tabasco and Worcestershire sauce to taste. Form into small balls. Roll in finely minced dried beef.

Chive-Cheese Balls: Mix 2 packages (6 ounces) cream cheese with ⅓ cup chopped chives, ¾ teaspoon French mustard, salt and pepper to taste. Form into tiny balls. Chill.

Cottage Cheese Balls: Blend dry cottage cheese with just enough milk or cream to form a smooth paste. Season with salt, pepper, and grated onion. Form into balls. Roll in chopped parsley. Chill.

Cream Cheese Balls: Shape cream cheese into tiny balls. Sprinkle with paprika or roll in finely chopped nuts or olives. Chill.

Cucumber Balls: With a ball vegetable cutter, cut large cucumbers into balls. Marinate in dressing. Sprinkle with paprika.

Green Balls: Mix together ½ cup grated Swiss cheese, ½ cup minced cooked ham, ½ teaspoon prepared mustard, 1 egg yolk, ¼ teaspoon salt, and a dash of pepper. Form in balls and roll in minced chives or parsley.

Liver Sausage Balls: Mix in a bowl which has been rubbed with a cut clove of garlic 1 cup liver sausage, ¼ cup finely chopped celery, and 2 tablespoons finely chopped green pepper. Form into balls and roll in finely chopped dill pickle.

Mix with grated raw carrot or ketchup and form into balls.

Roquefort-Cream Cheese Balls: Mix together Roquefort or blue cheese and cream cheese. Form into balls. Roll in chopped nuts. Chill.

Strawberries: Form cream cheese to resemble strawberries in shape. Roll in paprika. Stick pieces of parsley in the ends.

PICKLED COCKTAIL MUSHROOMS

2 (4-ounce) cans button mushrooms
1 cup white wine or cider vinegar
1 tablespoon sugar
1 teaspoon salt
1 shredded bay leaf
3 cloves
3 peppercorns
1 clove garlic, sliced
1 slice lemon

Combine vinegar, seasonings, and mushroom liquor. Boil 3 to 4 minutes. Add mushrooms. Turn into a jar and let stand overnight. Letting them stand from 1 to 2 weeks will improve the flavor. Serve whole on toothpicks or chop and use as a canapé spread.

GLAZED SHRIMP HORS D'OEUVRES #1

1 cup canned tomatoes
6 tablespoons water
2 tablespoons chopped celery
1 carrot, sliced
1 tablespoon chopped green
　pepper
1 whole clove

¼ teaspoon salt
⅛ teaspoon pepper
¾ tablespoon plain gelatin
1½ teaspoons lemon juice
1 pound fresh prepared
　shrimp, chilled

Put tomatoes and 4 tablespoons water in saucepan. Add vegetables and seasoning and bring to boiling point on high heat. Reduce heat and cook 15 minutes; strain. Soften gelatin in 2 tablespoons cold water 5 minutes. Add to hot tomato juice and stir until gelatin is dissolved. Stir in lemon juice. Chill in refrigerator until of syrupy consistency. Dip cold shrimp in gelatin mixture. Drain on cake rack and chill. Repeat several times to build up heavy coating of aspic on shrimp. To serve, place a glazed shrimp on a potato chip.

Glazed Shrimp Hors D'Oeuvres #2: Soak 2 teaspoons plain gelatin in ¼ cup cold water. Dissolve over boiling water. Add to 1 cup French dressing. Dip whole cooked or canned cleaned shrimp into glaze. Chill until glaze is firm.

CHEESE CARROTS #1

1 teaspoon plain gelatin
2 tablespoons cold water
½ cup smoked cheese spread

¼ teaspoon Worcestershire
　sauce
2 medium-sized carrots, grated
Parsley

Soften gelatin in cold water 5 minutes. Melt over hot water. Cool slightly. Blend with cheese and Worcestershire sauce. Place in refrigerator until of pliable consistency. Divide into 1 teaspoon portions. Shape into cones. Roll in grated carrots and stick sprig of parsley in large end to represent carrot top. Yield: about 30.

Cheese Carrots #2: To ½ cup soft, sharp-flavored cheese, add 1 tablespoon butter or margarine and ¼ teaspoon Worcestershire sauce. Form into shape of little carrots. Roll in fresh grated carrot. Make a small hole in the big end and insert a tiny piece of parsley for "leaves." Chill.

Herring Appetizer

HOMEMADE PICKLED HERRING

6 *matjes herring*	¼ *cup mixed pickling spices*
6 *milts from herring*	1 *cup vinegar*
6 *large onions, sliced*	½ *lemon, sliced (optional)*

Soak herring in water overnight. Clean, skin and bone, if desired. On a wooden board thoroughly pound the milt. Slice herring into 1-inch slices or leave whole. Place in jar in alternate layers with onion and lemon slices. Pour over vinegar mixed with spices and milt. Cover and keep in cool place three days. Will keep a week or longer. Serve cold.

Pickled herring with sour cream: In above recipe add ½ pint sour cream at the last.

HERRING IN WINE SAUCE

Clean herring and remove fins, tail, and head. Leave skin on. Cut into 1-inch pieces. Prepare marinade of equal parts vinegar, wine, and brown sugar. Add well mashed milt and a bay leaf for each herring. Place herring in glass jar and cover with marinade. Let stand several hours before serving.

SCANDINAVIAN PICKLED HERRING

2 *fat salted Iceland herring*	½ *cup sugar*
1 *medium-sized onion, finely chopped*	3 *bay leaves*
	¼ *teaspoon white pepper*
1 *cup white vinegar*	1 *teaspoon whole allspice*

Clean herring and soak in cold water overnight. Cut in halves, bone and skin. Cut into ½-inch strips. Arrange herring and onion in layers in serving dish. Mix vinegar, sugar, bay leaf, pepper, and allspice; add to herring. Let stand overnight. Serve chilled.

Wedges, Rolls, Cornucopias

BOLOGNA WEDGES

Put 2 or 3 thin slices of bologna together with a very thin layer of softened spicy cream cheese between each slice. Wrap in waxed paper. Chill thoroughly. To serve, cut into cubes or small wedges. Spear each with a pick.

Variations: Ham, tongue, or any desired luncheon meat may be substituted for bologna. For the filling use finely chopped hard-cooked egg mixed with mayonnaise and chopped pickle instead of cream cheese. Spear each wedge with a small pickled onion, if desired.

HAM AND SWISS CHEESE WEDGES

Have ham and Swiss cheese cut into very thin slices. Cream butter with horseradish-mustard and curry powder to taste. Spread a slice of ham with seasoned butter. Cover with slice of cheese. Spread with butter and continue in this way until stack is ½ inch thick. Wrap tightly in waxed paper. Chill thoroughly. To serve, cut into cubes or small wedges. Place 1 cube and pickled onion on each toothpick.

ROQUEFORT-MEAT WEDGES

⅓ cup Roquefort or blue cheese   1 tablespoon horseradish
2 tablespoons cream   12 thin slices bologna, salami, or
                                                             tongue

Blend cheese, cream, and horseradish. Spread meats with mixture. Make two 6-slice stacks. Do not spread top slices. Wrap in waxed paper. Chill thoroughly. To serve, cut into small wedges. Stick each with a pick.

VEAL AND CHEESE WEDGES

½ can veal loaf   Dash of cayenne or Tabasco
3-ounce package cream cheese   sauce
½ teaspoon grated onion   ½ teaspoon milk or cream
                                                       Salt to taste

Cut veal loaf into very thin slices. Cream the cheese, onion, cayenne or Tabasco with milk or cream until smooth. Add salt to taste.

Spread 3 slices of veal with cheese mixture. Stack and top with an unspread slice. Repeat until all ingredients have been used up. Wrap each stack in waxed paper. Chill thoroughly. To serve, cut into bite-size wedges or squares and serve on picks.

BOLOGNA-CHEESE RIBBONS

4 tablespoons cream cheese
1/4 teaspoon finely minced onion
1/8 teaspoon salt

1 teaspoon horseradish
3 1/16 inch slices large bologna
2 1/8-inch slices cheddar cheese

Blend together first 4 ingredients. Alternate slices of bologna with cheddar cheese, putting cream cheese mixture between slices; chill. When cheese is firm, cut into strips approximately 1/2 inch by 1 1/2 inches. Yield: about 16.

MEAT CORNUCOPIAS

These simple but tasty and decorative hors d'oeuvres can be made from a variety of ready-to-eat meats with varied fillings. Use thinly sliced boiled or baked ham, bologna, cervelat, or salami spread with a filling of highly seasoned cream cheese. Roll up cornucopia fashion and secure each with a pick. Garnish each with a tiny sprig of parsley or watercress, or a bit of pimiento. Other favorite combinations include chicken or turkey breast with chopped sweet pickle and dried beef with cream cheese. Other specific suggestions follow.

HAM CORNUCOPIAS

Slice cold baked or boiled ham very thin. Trim neatly into oblongs about 2 1/2 by 3 inches. Then roll lengthwise into small cornucopias and fasten each with a toothpick. Whip cream until stiff. Fold in horseradish to taste. Fill cornucopias with mixture and garnish with sprig of parsley inserted in open end of cornucopia.

MELON AND HAM CORNUCOPIAS

Wrap small chilled wedges of melon with very thin slices of ham. Fasten with picks. Use Italian prosciutto ham and honeydew melon.

CANAPE SALAD ROLLS

Remove crusts from thin slices of bread. Use several kinds: white, whole wheat, and rye. Spread each slice with 2 tablespoons of a finely chopped salad sandwich mixture. Roll up jelly-roll fashion. Wrap in waxed paper. Chill until serving time. Slice to serve.

CHICKEN ROLLS

Soften cream cheese with brandy. Season with salt. Spread thin slices of chicken. Roll up and fasten with toothpicks.

35

SALAMI CORNUCOPIAS

Spread thinly sliced salami with mustard. Roll and fasten with tooth-picks. Serve plain or place a small pickle or a stuffed olive in the center as a filling, or roll each around a few stalks of watercress.

SMOKED SALMON AND CHEESE ROLLS

Spread thin slices of smoked salmon with cream cheese seasoned with horseradish, salt, and black pepper. Roll up. Fasten with picks.

SMOKED SALMON-CAVIAR CORNUCOPIAS

Roll very thin slices of smoked salmon into cornucopias. Fasten with toothpicks. Fill each with caviar seasoned with lemon juice, or caviar mixed with riced hard-cooked eggs seasoned with lemon juice and paprika.

PUFF PASTE-CAVIAR CORNUCOPIAS

Roll puff paste very thin. Cut into small squares. Fold over caviar seasoned with lemon juice. Pinch edges together. Fry in deep hot fat.

BOLOGNA ROLLS

2 ounces cheddar cheese	6 slices large bologna
2 teaspoons softened butter	4 large stuffed olives, cut into
1 large stuffed olive, chopped fine	lengthwise strips

Cream the cheese and butter together. Stir in chopped olive. Spread each round of bologna with 2½ teaspoons of cheese mixture. Cut rounds crosswise into 4 triangular parts. Beginning at point of tri-angle, roll and secure with toothpick. Garnish ends of roll with slice of olive. Chill. Yield: 24.

SMITHFIELD HAM ROLLS

Spread thin slices of Smithfield ham with cottage cheese mixed with piccalilli. Roll up. Fasten with picks.

HAM AND OLIVE PINWHEELS

3 slices boiled ham	2 tablespoons olive-pimento
About 12 small stuffed olives	cheese spread

Spread each slice of ham with 2 teaspoons cheese spread. Cut into ¾-inch strips. Place an olive at end of each strip and roll. Secure with toothpick and chill. When cheese is firm, remove toothpicks and cut each roll in half to form 2 pinwheels. Serve with cut side up. Yield: about 24.

Serve Yourself Canapé Spread Tray

ASPARAGUS ROLLS #1

Cut fresh bread in very thin slices and remove crusts. Spread with mustard or mayonnaise. Roll each slice around an asparagus tip. Fasten with toothpicks. Place in shallow pan and cover with damp cloth. Chill thoroughly. Remove toothpicks before serving.

Asparagus Rolls #2: Season mayonnaise with dry mustard to taste. Spread on small slices of tongue. Roll each slice around an asparagus tip. Secure with a toothpick.

HAM ROLLS

Spread thin evenly shaped slices of boiled or baked ham with a mixture of prepared mustard and mayonnaise. Cut as many thin strips of bread as there are rolls to be made. Place a bread strip on the end of each ham slice and roll ham over it very tightly. Dip sprigs of parsley or watercress in French dressing and insert 1 or 2 sprigs in each roll. Fasten the rolls with picks and keep in cold place until serving time.

DRIED BEEF WHIRLIGIGS

Dried beef slices
3-ounce package cream cheese
⅛ teaspoon finely chopped garlic

¼ teaspoon finely chopped onion
1 tablespoon blue cheese
½ teaspoon Worcestershire sauce

Place 2 slices of dried beef together, overlapping slightly. Beat the cream cheese with remaining ingredients and spread on beef slices. Roll up jelly-roll fashion. Chill, then cut diagonally with a very sharp knife into ¼-inch slices. Serve on picks. Yield: about 36.

Canape Spreads

CHEESE CANAPE SPREADS

Camembert or Liederkranz Spread: Blend Camembert or Liederkranz cheese with half as much cream cheese.

Cottage Cheese Spread: Mix 1 cup cottage cheese with 4 tablespoons melted butter and ½ teaspoon each of onion juice and lemon juice. Add salt, pepper, and paprika to taste. Garnish the spread canapé bases with slices of stuffed olive or strips of pimiento or bell pepper.

Cheese-Wine-Olive Spread: Combine aged American or cheddar cheese with enough sherry wine to make a smooth spread. Add half as much chopped stuffed olives. Mix well.

Cheese-Olive Spread #1: Put 2 parts American cheese and 1 part stuffed or pitted olives through the meat grinder using a fine knife. Mix together well.

Cheese-Olive Spread #2: Combine ¼ cup grated soft, sharp cheese, ¼ cup butter, and add ¼ cup finely chopped green or stuffed olives. Season to taste with salt and pepper.

Cheese-Pickle Spread: Combine 1 cup grated American cheese and ½ cup well-drained chopped dill pickle. Moisten with 1 tablespoon ketchup and 2 tablespoons mayonnaise.

Roquefort-Watercress Spread: Soften 8 ounces Roquefort or other blue cheese and blend thoroughly with ¼ cup finely minced watercress. Season with salt and pepper to taste and add 1 teaspoon Worcestershire sauce.

Roquefort Spread: Combine ¼ cup Roquefort or blue cheese with 2 tablespoons cream cheese, and 1 tablespoon mayonnaise. Season with a few drops of Worcestershire sauce.

Roquefort-Chives Spread: Mix Roquefort cheese with enough French dressing to moisten. Season with chopped chives.

CREAM CHEESE CANAPE SPREADS

Cheese-Watercress Spread: Cream 1 package (3 ounces) cream cheese. Dry and chop 1 cup watercress. Blend together with 1 teaspoon Worcestershire sauce and ¼ teaspoon salt.

Chili-Cheese Spread: Combine 1 package (3 ounces) cream cheese or ½ cup grated American cheese with enough chili sauce to moisten.

Orange-Cream Cheese Spread: Mix 1 package (3 ounces) cream cheese, grated rind of 1 orange, ¼ teaspoon salt, and ⅛ teaspoon paprika. Spread on buttered bases and top with chopped toasted pecan meats.

Cheese-Onion Spread: Soften cream cheese with cream. Add a few drops onion juice or minced onion. Season with salt and pepper. Garnish with paprika or minced parsley.

Cream Cheese-Pickle Spread: Mix finely chopped pickles with cream cheese. Garnish with slices of stuffed olives.

Cheese-Sour Cream Spread: Blend cream cheese with sour cream. Season with salt and pepper.

Garlic-Cream Cheese Spread: Rub a salad bowl with a cut clove of garlic. Moisten cream cheese with a bit of cream and work in the bowl until cheese is softened and has absorbed some of the garlic flavor. Garnish with finely minced parsley.

Cheese-Green Pepper Spread: Blend 1 package (3 ounces) cream cheese with 4 tablespoons minced green pepper, 2 tablespoons minced onion, 1 teaspoon French dressing, and a few grains of cayenne.

Cheese-Nut Spread: Blend cream cheese with chopped nuts and sweeten to taste with confectioners' sugar.

Cheese-Caviar Spread: Moisten cream cheese with cream. Spread on small crackers. Dot with caviar.

COCKTAIL CHEESE BALL

2 3-ounce *packages cream cheese*
1½ *ounces Roquefort cheese*
1 *jar (5 ounces) smoked cheese spread*
1 *teaspoon Worcestershire sauce*

1 *tablespoon minced onion*
1 *tablespoon minced stuffed olives*
2 *tablespoons minced parsley*
½ *cup finely chopped walnuts*

Combine all ingredients except parsley and nuts. Blend thoroughly. Chill overnight. Shape into ball. Roll in parsley and nuts. Serve surrounded with potato chips and crackers.

CHEESE LOG

3-ounce package cream cheese
3 ounces soft butter
1 teaspoon capers
1 teaspoon paprika

½ teaspoon caraway seed
½ teaspoon anchovy paste
1 tablespoon minced onion

Blend all ingredients. Shape into roll. Wrap in waxed paper. Chill thoroughly. Let your guests cut and spread it on crackers, melba toast, or thinly sliced bread.

COCKTAIL CHEESE MOLD

2 3-ounce packages cream cheese
¼ cup soft butter
½ teaspoon caraway seed
1 tablespoon anchovy paste

1 teaspoon paprika
1 tablespoon chopped chives
½ teaspoon salt
1 teaspoon capers

Cream the cheese and butter together until fluffy. Add remaining ingredients and mix well. Pack into small mold. Chill several hours. Unmold on tray or plate. Serve with potato chips and crackers.

FISH AND SEAFOOD CANAPE SPREADS

Anchovy-Cheese Spread: Combine 1 part anchovy paste with 2 parts cream cheese. Spread and garnish with minced egg yolk.

Anchovy-Egg Spread: Mash and blend 4 hard-cooked egg yolks and 4 anchovies. Moisten to spreading consistency with mayonnaise. Season with grated onion and black pepper. Spread and garnish with chopped egg white.

Caviar Spread #1: Flavor caviar with onion juice and lemon juice. Spread and decorate with tiny pearl onions.

Caviar Spread #2: Mash yolks of 3 hard-cooked eggs. Blend with ⅓ cup creamed butter and ⅓ cup caviar.

Chopped Herring Spread: Wash, clean, bone, and chop salted herring which has been soaked in cold water for several hours. For each herring use 1 onion, 1 sour apple, 1 slice of toast soaked in vinegar or lemon juice. Chop all together very fine and add 1 teaspoon salad oil, a dash each of cinnamon and pepper. Serve garnished with finely chopped hard-cooked egg.

Crabmeat or Lobster Spread: Make a paste of canned or cooked seafood. Moisten with mayonnaise. Season with lemon juice and grated onion.

Crabmeat or Lobster and Deviled Egg Spread: Drain, bone, and wash contents of 1 can (6 ounces) seafood. Mash with 2 hard-cooked eggs, ½ teaspoon mustard, 2 tablespoons mayonnaise, 1 tablespoon lemon juice, and about 1 teaspoon curry powder.

Kippered Herring Spread: Combine 1 cup mashed kippered herring with 1 chopped hard-cooked egg and ¼ cup minced cucumber. Moisten with mayonnaise and season with 2 drops lemon juice.

Sardine Spread #1: Mash and blend together 3 sardines and 1 package (3 ounces) cream cheese. Season with lemon juice to taste.

Sardine Spread #2: Drain oil from 1 can sardines. Mash sardines and season with ½ tablespoon lemon juice, a few drops of Worcestershire sauce, salt and pepper to taste. Add enough butter to form a smooth paste.

Sardine Spread #3: Drain oil from 1 can sardines. Mash sardines with fork. Add 1 tablespoon mayonnaise, 1 tablespoon lemon juice, and ¼ teaspoon Tabasco sauce. Mix to a smooth paste.

Sardine and Hard-Cooked Egg Spread: Combine mashed sardines with mashed hard-cooked egg yolk. Season to taste with lemon juice. Add enough butter to form a smooth paste. Spread on toasted canapé bases. Garnish with riced white of egg. Sprinkle with chopped parsley.

Shrimp Spread: Combine ½ cup cut-up cleaned cooked or canned shrimp, 1 package (3 ounces) cream cheese, and 1½ teaspoons anchovy paste.

Shrimp and Pecan Spread: Grind and mix thoroughly equal parts smoked shrimp and pecan meats.

Smoked Salmon-Egg Spread: Chop or grind ½ pound smoked salmon. Add and blend 1 tablespoon olive oil, dash of paprika, and ½ teaspoon lemon juice. Mince yolks and whites of 2 hard-cooked eggs. Spread salmon mixture on canapé bases. Sprinkle with yolks, then with whites in circles.

Smoked Salmon and Mayonnaise Spread: Chop smoked salmon and combine with chopped hard-cooked eggs. Add mayonnaise and paprika.

Tuna or Salmon Spread: Make a paste from cooked or canned salmon or tuna. Moisten with mayonnaise and add lemon juice to taste. Spread and decorate with minced parsley.

Sturgeon-Cheese Spread: Combine 1 cup flaked kippered sturgeon (or herring), 1½ cups grated cheddar cheese, and ½ medium-sized

Bermuda onion, grated. Spread and garnish with slices of stuffed olives.

QUICK AND EASY FLAKED FISH CANAPE SPREADS

Cook, cool and flake fish fillets or use canned flaked fish. Then:

1. Mix equal quantities of flaked fish and chopped pearl onions, mix with mayonnaise and chili sauce. Serve on whole wheat crackers.

2. Mix equal quantities of flaked fish and chopped mustard pickle. Serve on crackers or toast strips.

3. Moisten flaked fish with cream and horseradish. Serve on crackers or toast strips, garnished with green pepper.

FRUIT AND VEGETABLE CANAPE SPREADS

Avocado Spread: Pare avocados and mash pulp with a fork. Season with lemon or lime juice and salt. Spread on canapé base and garnish with minced parsley.

Avocado-Egg Spread: Mash and blend equal parts of avocado pulp and hard-cooked egg yolk. Season with lemon juice and salt to taste.

Avocado-Olive Spread: Mix 1 cup mashed avocado pulp with ¼ cup finely chopped ripe or green olives. Season with lemon or lime juice. Spread on canapé base. Garnish with paprika, curled anchovies, pimiento strips, or red radish rounds.

Avocado-Onion Spread: Season mashed avocado pulp with minced onion, salt, and a dash of Tabasco sauce. Place a slice of tomato on canapé base and cover with spread.

Mushroom Spread: Wash and chop or grind mushrooms fine. Fry gently in butter for 5 minutes. Cool and season to taste with lemon juice, salt, and pepper.

Onion-Egg Spread: Chop 1 large onion fine. Add about 4 tablespoons melted chicken fat, 1 hard-cooked egg, chopped fine, and salt to taste.

Pickled Beet and Egg Spread: Combine equal parts of finely minced pickled beets and minced hard-cooked eggs. Season to taste.

MUSHROOM CANAPE SPREAD #2

4-ounce can mushrooms (use pieces and stems)	Onion juice to taste
4 tablespoons butter	Salt and pepper to taste
¼ cup heavy cream	¾ cup English cheddar cheese

Drain mushrooms. Sauté in butter. Add cream, seasonings, and cheese. Mash to a paste. Spread toast rounds or squares with a softened butter, then spread with mushroom mixture. Sprinkle with paprika.

EGGPLANT BIARRITZ

1 medium-sized eggplant
2 medium-sized onions, minced
1 green pepper, minced
¼ cup olive oil (about)
¼ teaspoon oregano

1 can (2½ cups) tomatoes
1 large clove garlic, chopped fine
1 teaspoon salt (about)
⅛ teaspoon pepper

Cut eggplant in half. Boil in water to cover until tender (about 20 minutes). Sauté onions and green pepper in oil until brown. Add garlic. Peel eggplant and mash pulp and seeds with a fork. Add to onions with tomatoes and seasonings. Simmer on a very low flame 20 to 30 minutes. Let cool, if desired. Serve hot or cold on squares of pumpernickel or rye bread.

EGGPLANT CAVIAR

1 eggplant
2 small onions, minced
2 cloves, minced
1 clove garlic, minced

1 ripe tomato, peeled and minced
Salt and pepper
Vinegar
Olive oil

Broil the whole eggplant over direct flame or in a broiler for 15 to 20 minutes. Remove the inside pulp and mix with the onions, cloves, and garlic. Add the tomato and season to taste with salt, pepper, vinegar, and oil. Serve on greens, garnished with quartered tomatoes and black olives or use as spread on rye or pumpernickel bread.

MEAT CANAPE SPREADS

Chicken-Ham-Olive Spread: Combine ½ cup chopped cooked chicken, ½ cup chopped cooked ham, and ¼ cup chopped green olives. Moisten with mayonnaise.

Chicken Liver Spread: Combine ½ cup chopped cooked chicken livers with 1 or 2 hard-cooked eggs, finely chopped, and 1 teaspoon finely chopped onion. Season to taste with salt and pepper. Moisten with butter or chicken fat.

Chicken or Turkey Spread: Chop or grind cooked chicken or turkey. Moisten with mayonnaise. Add finely chopped celery. Season to taste. Garnish with watercress.

Chopped Liver and Egg Spread: Grind or chop very fine, ½ pound fried chicken livers, 1 hard-cooked egg, 1 small stalk celery, and 1 small onion. Moisten with melted chicken fat or butter. Add salt and pepper to taste. Mix to a smooth paste.

Chopped Liver and Mushroom Spread: Chop fine ½ pound fried chicken or calves' livers. Sauté ½ cup fresh mushrooms for 5 minutes in 3 tablespoons of chicken fat or butter. Chop fine and add both mushrooms and the fat in which they were fried to the liver. Season to taste with salt, pepper, and onion juice.

Deviled Ham Spread #1: Combine ¼ cup deviled ham, 1 tablespoon finely chopped celery, and 1 chopped hard-cooked egg. Combine ¼ teaspoon curry powder and ½ teaspoon olive oil. Add to ham mixture and moisten with mayonnaise. Add salt to taste.

Deviled Ham Spread #2: Blend equal parts of deviled ham and creamed butter. Season with mustard to taste.

Deviled Ham and Cheese Spread: Combine 6 ounces deviled ham with ¼ cup pimiento cheese spread and 2 tablespoons chopped sweet pickle. Moisten with mayonnaise.

Dried Beef-Cheese-Almond Spread: Combine 1 cup chopped dried beef and ½ cup each of pineapple cheese and chopped toasted almonds. Season with 2 tablespoons lemon juice.

Ham-Cheese Spread: Combine 1 cup finely chopped cooked ham, ¼ cup grated American cheese, ½ teaspoon finely chopped onion, and 1 teaspoon chili sauce.

Liverwurst Spread: Mash ½ cup liverwurst to a paste. Season with 2 tablespoons horseradish and ½ teaspoon prepared mustard.

Liverwurst and Bacon Spread: Chop cold crisp bacon very fine. Combine 1 part bacon with 3 parts liverwurst. Season with salt, pepper, Worcestershire sauce and Tabasco sauce to taste.

Minced Ham Spread: Moisten finely ground cooked ham with mayonnaise. Add a little chopped dill pickle or sweet pickle relish.

Pate de Foie Gras Spread: Mix 3 tablespoons of pâté de foie gras, ¼ cup cream, and salt and pepper to taste. Force the mixture through a sieve.

Mock Pate de Foie Gras Spread: Fry 1 ounce salt pork until crisp. Grind with 8 ounces cooked chicken livers. Season with lemon juice, salt, and pepper. Moisten with mayonnaise.

Roast Beef or Veal Spreads: Moisten finely ground meat with mixture of horseradish and mayonnaise. Season to taste.

Tongue, Corned Beef, Bologna, or Salami Spreads: Moisten finely ground cooked meat with mayonnaise. Add a little finely chopped sweet pickle and pimiento. Season to taste.

BRAUNSCHWEIGER PINEAPPLE CENTERPIECE

Use 1½ to 2 pounds cold, firm Braunschweiger sausage. Remove covering and mold it into shape of a fresh pineapple. Brush with a little lemon juice or soft butter. Cover surface with slices of stuffed olive to resemble "eyes" of pineapple. Top with 3 or 4 green onions or leaves from fresh pineapple. Serve surrounded with crackers and potato chips.

LIEDERKRANZ CANAPE SPREAD

4 ounces soft Liederkranz cheese
½ cup soft butter
½ teaspoon salt
¼ teaspoon pepper
⅛ teaspoon paprika
½ teaspoon prepared mustard
¼ teaspoon Worcestershire sauce
3 tablespoons minced green pepper
2 tablespoons minced onion

Cream the cheese until smooth and fluffy. Gradually blend in butter. Blend in remaining ingredients. Serve with thin slices of rye or pumpernickel bread.

DRIED BEEF AVOCADO WHIP

1 ripe avocado
¼ teaspoon salt
Juice of ½ lemon
⅓ cup frizzled dried beef

Slice avocado in half lengthwise. Remove seed and scoop out pulp carefully so that shells may be used as natural containers for the whipped spread. Mash the pulp and add salt, lemon juice, and frizzled beef. (To frizzle beef, brown in butter in heavy skillet until crisp.) Mix well and heap into shells.

CHICKEN LIVERS AND GIZZARDS SPREAD

4 chicken gizzards
1 medium onion, minced
8 chicken livers
3 tablespoons chicken fat
2 hard-cooked eggs
1 teaspoon parsley, minced
Salt and pepper

Simmer gizzards until tender. Fry chopped onion in chicken fat until lightly brown; add and saute livers and cooked gizzards. Chop eggs, gizzards, livers, and onions; add seasoning, parsley, and some chicken fat. Force this through a sieve and serve cold.

Miscellaneous Cold Canapes

AVOCADO CANAPES

1 medium-sized avocado
1 tablespoon onion juice
1 tablespoon lemon juice
¼ teaspoon salt
Dash of Tabasco sauce

2 tablespoons mayonnaise
Tomato slices
Toast rounds
Stuffed olives

Pare and pit the avocado. Mash pulp with a fork; add onion juice, lemon juice, salt, and Tabasco sauce. Moisten with mayonnaise and spread on toast rounds. Top each with a thin slice of tomato. Put a small mound of avocado mixture in the center. Garnish with sliced olives.

CRAB CANAPES

1 cup flaked crabmeat
2 hard-cooked eggs, chopped
1 teaspoon lemon juice
3 tablespoons mayonnaise
½ teaspoon Worcestershire
  sauce

Dash of Tabasco sauce
Salt and pepper
Ripe olives or capers
Cream cheese

Mix crabmeat with chopped egg and seasonings. Cut bread with diamond-shaped cutter; toast and spread with soft butter and crab mixture. Decorate with cream cheese (blend ⅓ cup cream cheese with 2 tablespoons mayonnaise, and ¼ teaspoon Worcestershire sauce) and put through pastry bag. Garnish. Yield: 24 canapés.

SALAMI CANAPES

½ pound hard salami
3 hard-cooked eggs
½ cup salad dressing

Bread, sliced thin
Parsley
Pimiento

Put salami and hard-cooked eggs through food chopper 2 or 3 times. Blend with salad dressing. Trim crust from bread and cut into small squares. Toast on one side. Spread untoasted side with salami mixture. Sprinkle with chopped parsley and garnish with pimiento strips.

LOBSTER CANAPES

3 tablespoons lobster paste
3 tablespoons butter
6 small rounds of toast

2 hard-cooked eggs
3 stuffed olives

Cream together the lobster paste and butter. Spread evenly on toast rounds. Arrange thick slices of hard-cooked egg in center. Cut olives in halves and press a half into the center of egg slices, cut side up.

SHRIMP AND AVOCADO CANAPES

Peel and mash a small avocado. Season with 1 teaspoon lemon juice, 1 teaspoon minced onion, and a dash of salt. Spread on crackers and top each with a whole shrimp.

SMOKED SALMON CANAPES #1

Trim crusts from thinly sliced bread. Cut in strips. Toast on one side. Spread untoasted side with Lemon Butter. Brush edges with mayonnaise and dip in chopped parsley. Place a wafer-thin slice of smoked salmon on each. Garnish with chopped hard-cooked egg white and chopped parsley.

SMOKED SALMON CANAPES #2

Chop 2 hard-cooked egg whites very fine. Mix with ½ teaspoon grated onion, salt and pepper to taste, and mayonnaise for spreading consistency. Spread on buttered toast. Place sliced olive in center and strips of salmon at each end.

SMOKED SALMON CANAPES #3

Split small hard rolls. Spread with cream cheese. Top with thinly sliced smoked salmon. Cut into bite-size wedges.

Hot Kabobs

A FEW of the many and varied combinations which could be termed kabobs are given below. Some hostesses like the idea of a "broil-your-own" kabob party. For such a party you would have to have on hand a supply of metal skewers and/or some sturdy twigs whittled to a sharp point. The kabobs are held over coals, small cans of lighted Sterno, or little spirit lamps (the little glass ones with wicks used by chemists) and they are rotated slowly until the food is "done to a turn." A nice effect is obtained by placing small lamps in the centers of hollowed-out heads of cabbage with the lamps hidden and only the flames showing. Any of the tender meats, seafoods, and many combinations suggested for the broiler may be selected as long as you bear in mind that they must be foods that cook quickly. Suggestions include tiny sausages or cubes of sausage, cubes of ham, tender steak, lamb, kidney, shrimp, oysters, whole button mushrooms, tiny onions, and so forth. Let your imagination rule the choice of additional fruits and vegetables to alternate with the tender meats on the skewers. Be sure to stick a cork or an olive on each metal skewer to protect your guests' fingers.

MUSHROOM AND FRANK KABOBS

Place small canned mushrooms and 1-inch pieces of frankfurter on picks. Brush with melted butter. Broil.

BROILED HAM AND PINEAPPLE KABOBS

Place chunks of pineapple and cubes of ham on picks. Brush with corn syrup. Broil until golden brown.

HOT COCKTAIL SAUSAGES

Broil or sauté cocktail-size sausages. If larger ones are used, cut into 1-inch lengths. Spear each with a pick.

BROILED FRUIT BITS

Roll in small bacon strips, 1-inch squares of watermelon, peach, pear, or any spiced fruit. Fasten with a pick and broil.

PEARL ONION KABOBS

Wrap pearl onions in small strips of bacon. Fasten with picks. Broil until bacon is crisp.

BACONETTES

Spread small slices of uncooked bacon with peanut butter. Roll tightly. Fasten with picks. Broil until bacon is done. Replace picks if they are burnt.

HOT BACON ROLLS IN VARIETY

Wrap small strips of bacon around combinations of any of the following: ham cubes, stuffed olives, tiny pickles, cooked shrimp, stuffed prunes, cocktail frankfurters or other sausage, or small button mushrooms. Fasten with picks. Broil until bacon is done.

BROILED CHICKEN LIVERS

Cut chicken livers into serving size pieces. Broil and sprinkle with onion juice to taste, or sauté in chicken fat and season to taste. Spear each with a pick.

BACON SCALLOPS

Parboil scallops in their own liquor for 3 minutes. Drain and dry with paper towels. Cut scallops into bite-size pieces. Wrap each in a piece of bacon. Fasten with a pick. Broil or bake in a hot oven until bacon is crisp. Serve hot with a bowl of cocktail sauce.

SHRIMP KABOB

Alternate on a skewer whole shrimp, tomato wedges, okra, and bacon. Broil until done.

HOT SHRIMP AND PINEAPPLE KABOBS

Marinate cooked, cleaned shrimp in soy sauce. Spear a small whole shrimp and a cube of canned pineapple on each pick. Bake or broil until hot.

CERVELAT KABOBS

Cervelat
Small boiled onions

Canned button mushrooms
Melted butter

Cut the cervelat into small thick cubes. Thread alternating cubes of cervelat, small boiled onions, and small button mushrooms on skewers. Brush with melted butter. Broil until hot and slightly browned. These make hearty hors d'oeuvres. If the cervelat is cut into larger size cubes this combination may be used for a quick lunch or dinner dish with ½ pound cervelat, 5 onions, and 10 mushrooms serving 55.

SHISH KEBAB FOR HORS D'OEUVRES

¼ cup olive oil
1 teaspoon salt
¼ teaspoon pepper
2 tablespoons wine (optional)
2 pounds lean lamb, cut into small cubes
3 small firm tomatoes, cut into wedges

3 small onions, cut into thick slices
Small whole mushrooms
1 large green pepper, cut into small squares
Cubed eggplant

Combine olive oil, pepper, salt, and wine. Spread over meat and vegetables. Let stand in cool place 2 to 3 hours. Place meat and vegetables alternately on skewers. If desired, rub skewers first with cut clove of garlic. Broil slowly under moderate heat until tender, turning to brown all sides.

CHICKEN LIVERS EN BROCHETTE

Cut livers in bite-size pieces. Cut sliced bacon in 1-inch pieces. Fill skewers with alternate pieces of chicken liver, bacon, and small button mushrooms. Dip in melted butter and roll in bread crumbs. Broil under moderate heat until browned on all sides. Season with salt and pepper.

HAWAIIAN TERIYAKI

1 pound tender beefsteak
¼ cup soy sauce
1 tablespoon sugar

1 clove garlic, minced
1 teaspoon fresh ginger, minced

Slice meat across grain into thin strips. Place on bamboo sticks. (They can be bought in Chinese stores.) Mix soy, sugar, garlic, and ginger. Soak meat in sauce 30 minutes or longer, turning to marinate evenly. Broil 5 minutes on each side. Serve hot.

Cheeses

CHEESE TRAYS

Cheese trays offer limitless possibilities for variety both in the choice of cheeses and the foods accompanying them. Cheeses are world-wide favorites for snacks because cheese is one of the friendliest of foods, mixing well in many ways. In making up a tray, provide an assortment of cheeses together with a variety of breads and crackers as well as some of the suggested fruits. And remember that some of your guests like butter with their cheese.

CHEESE GUIDE

American Cheddar: Colored or natural. Firm to crumbly in texture. Mild to sharp in flavor. A favorite to serve on snack trays, with crackers, fruit, cobblers, pies, in sandwiches, creamy sauces, and in omelets.

Bel Paese: Light yellow. Mellow flavor. Soft to solid consistency. Delicious with plain crackers or with fruit for dessert.

Blue: Includes French Roquefort and Bleu, America and Danish Blue, English Stilton, and Italian Gorgonzola. All are marbled with blue-green mold, have a mild to sharp, sort of pungent salty flavor. Use for canapé spreads and snacks or crumbled in crunchy salads and in salad dressings. Particularly delicious with fresh pears or toasted unsalted crackers and sherry.

Brick: Creamy white. Has small eyes and an elastic texture. Mild to sharp flavor. Use on cheese trays, with crackers, and in sandwiches.

Brie: Soft, creamy interior with light russet-brown crust. Pronounced odor. Sharp flavor. Spread it, crust and all, on crackers, dark whole-grain breads, on French bread, or on slices of unpeeled apple.

Camembert: Soft, creamy, yellowish interior with a thin, whitish crust. Rich, mild flavor. To serve, soften it at room temperature. At its peak its interior will be like thick cream. World-wide favorite dessert cheese. Spread it, crust and all, on slices of unpeeled apple, on crackers plain or toasted, and on French bread.

Chantelle: Robust American cheese with a shiny red coat, a semi-soft, creamy yellow interior. Mellow flavor. Use on cheese trays, for snacks, sandwiches, and for dessert. Serve wedges with apples, pears, or pineapple.

Cottage: White, mild, uncured. There are two types: Pot type is the plain curd of skimmed milk; cottage type has cream added. Use plain in salads or spreads, or mixed with chives, nutmeats, pickle relish, diced fruit, etc. The dry type is frequently called for in certain recipes.

Cream: White, delicately flavored and fresh as cream. Soft texture. Thin with cream to top fruit salads and desserts or for spreads. Particularly good as a sandwich filling with date and nut breads. Cube it for fruit salads. Season and form into balls for hors d'oeuvres.

Edam or Gouda: Round cheeses with flattened ends and red coatings. Mild flavor which is sometimes salty and nut-like. Gouda weighs less than a pound. Edam weighs 2 to 4 pounds. Use as a hub for a snack or dessert tray. They are pretty to look at and the mild flavor blends well with tart apples, grapes, and tangerines.

Gjetost: Dark brown. Smooth textured. Full sweet flavor. Slice thin and serve with crackers or raisin bread.

Liederkranz: Golden yellow with a hearty, robust flavor. Odor somewhat resembles Limburger. Soft, creamy spreading consistency. Serve with toast, crackers, rye, and pumpernickel breads. The thin crust should be eaten for fullest enjoyment.

Limburger: Soft textured. Characteristic odor and flavor. Despite the fact that there is so much jesting about it Limburger is among the most delicious of cheese flavors. Serve the same way as Liederkranz.

Münster: Orange-colored rind with light-yellow interior full of tiny holes. Often flavored with anise or caraway seed. Has a semi-hard texture. Serve with vegetable relish tray. Good with scallions, cucumbers, carrot sticks, radishes, etc. Excellent with pumpernickel bread or date-nut bread.

Parmesan: Rich yellow color. Mild to full flavor. Texture is firm to hard—usually the latter. Grate to serve on spaghetti, soups like minestrone and onion, on salads and casseroles.

Pineapple: Named for its shape. Yellow to orange color. Molded from American cheese and has similar flavor. Use as centerpiece in a tray. Hollow out cone-shaped piece in center; cut in cubes and return to shell. Serve with cocktail picks.

Port Salut: Delicate in flavor. It has a moderately soft interior but it slices well. Serve with plain bland crackers or all by itself. Good either way.

Provolone: A smoky-tasting cheese that comes in several shapes. It is commonly seen hanging in ball shapes or long cylindrical forms in Italian grocery stores. Excellent with rye or whole-wheat crackers.

Swiss-Emmenthal: Pale yellow hard cheese with round rather large holes. Has a nut-like sweet flavor. Slice thin to serve on platters with other foods. Use with rye breads or serve in small sticks with salad plates. Gruyère, another Swiss cheese, can be bought in small packaged wedges as well as in bulk. The flavor is mild.

Processed Cheeses: They come in a number of flavors which include American (white and yellow), Brick, Pimiento, Olive-Pimiento, Limburger, Swiss, Caraway, etc. They have smooth, creamy textures. They spread easily and slice well when chilled. They melt smoothly and quickly. Use for snack and dessert trays, for cheese sauce, in soufflés, and other cheese cookery.

Cheese-Flavored Spreads: They include a variety of cheese spreads and cheese blends with a soft spreading consistency.

Smoked Cheeses: Processed cheese foods that are hickory-smoked or have smoke-flavored solids added. Serve sliced or cubed as an appetizer or snack. Some spread easily.

Hot Cheese Canapes
and Hors d'oeuvres

THE judicious use of cheese in many forms makes for a fascinating array of hot tidbits. Most of them take a little effort and watching after your guests have arrived. That work, however, may be cut down to a minimum if you remember that many may be prepared in advance and stored in the refrigerator until you are ready to give them the final touch. Moderate heat gives the best results in cheese cookery unless otherwise indicated as in recipes where biscuit dough or pastry is used.

APPETIZER PUFFS

Soften one 8-ounce package of cream cheese at room temperature and cream it until it is soft. Add 1 teaspoon grated onion, ½ teaspoon baking powder, 1 egg yolk, and salt and pepper to taste. Blend all ingredients thoroughly. Toast 18 small bread rounds. Spread two 2½-ounce cans of deviled meat on the bread rounds. Place a heaping spoonful of the cream cheese mixture on top of the deviled meat. Place in a moderate oven (375° F.) until heated through, lightly browned, and puffy, about 8 to 10 minutes.

HAM AND CHEESE PUFFS

1 cup ground cooked ham
3 tablespoons minced green pepper
1 tablespoon prepared mustard
¼ teaspoon Worcestershire sauce
½ cup thick white sauce

1 package (3 ounces) cream cheese
1 beaten egg yolk
1 teaspoon grated onion
¼ teaspoon baking powder
18 2-inch toast rounds

Combine ham, green pepper, mustard, and Worcestershire sauce. Stir in white sauce and mix well. Combine cheese, egg yolk, onion, and baking powder. Spread toast rounds with ham mixture. Top with cheese mixture. Broil under moderate heat until topping puffs and browns. Serve hot.

QUICK CHEESE PIZZA #1

6 English muffins
3 ripe tomatoes or 1¼ cups drained stewed tomatoes
24 anchovy fillets or dash of rosemary

12 thin slices of cheese
Olive oil
Salt and pepper

Break muffins apart. Toast until slightly crispy. Thinly slice tomatoes and place 1 slice or 2 tablespoons stewed tomatoes on each muffin half. Add either 2 anchovy fillets or dash of rosemary. Add another layer of fresh tomato or stewed tomatoes and top with slice of cheese. Sprinkle with olive oil, salt, and pepper. Place under broiler and broil until cheese melts.

Quick Cheese Pizza #2: Break the muffins apart. Spread with mayonnaise. Top with tomato slices. Sprinkle with grated Parmesan cheese. Add 2 or 3 anchovy fillets to each. Broil until muffins are toasted.

DELUXE CHEESE DREAMS

½ pound sharp cheese, grated
3-ounce package cream cheese
2 tablespoons butter, melted
1 egg, beaten

1 tablespoon cream
1 whole loaf white bread (unsliced)

Combine grated cheese with softened cream cheese, melted butter, and beaten egg, adding cream to moisten. Slice bread lengthwise or crosswise of loaf, as preferred. Spread lengthwise slices with the cheese mixture. Roll up like jelly roll and slice ⅜ inch thick. Spread thin crosswise slices with the mixture and roll from corner to corner, fastening with toothpick. (Sliced bread may be cut in rounds or other shapes and spread with cheese mixture, if desired.) Toast under broiler until golden brown. Serve hot. Yield: 2½ to 3 dozen.

QUICK CHEESE STRAWS

1 *cup prepared biscuit flour*   1 *cup grated American cheese*
Ice water

Add just enough water to the flour to make the dough stick together. Roll out to ¼-inch thickness. Spread with cheese. Fold dough over cheese and roll again. Repeat until cheese is all folded in. Chill. Roll thin and cut into strips. Bake in hot oven (400° F.) 15 minutes. Yield: about 4 dozen strips, 4 inches long.

· CHEESE STICKS

Cut bread into thin strips, lengthwise. Spread with butter. Sprinkle with grated cheese and season with salt and cayenne. Bake until delicately browned in moderate oven (350° F.). Sprinkle with finely minced ripe olives and serve.

HOT CHEESED CHICKEN CANAPES

Whip a small jar of nippy cheese spread until creamy. Add an equal amount of boned canned chicken or turkey. Season with Worcestershire sauce. Mix lightly but do not mash. Spread on cocktail crackers. Place on baking sheet. Bake in very hot oven (450° F.) or broil until cheese melts, about 5 minutes. Serve hot.

Quick Cheese Pizza Snacks

HOT CHEESED FRANK CANAPES

Simmer frankfurters until thoroughly heated. Drain and remove casings. Put through food chopper, using medium blade. Season to taste with prepared mustard. Add a little piccalilli and enough mayonnaise to give spreading consistency. Spread on toasted bread bases. Sprinkle with grated cheddar cheese. Just before serving, heat under moderate broiler until cheese melts. Serve hot. If desired, the frankfurter mixture may be used as a cold spread.

PARMESAN TOAST

Moisten Parmesan cheese with cream. Spread on toast or crackers. Bake in moderate oven until cheese melts.

SIMPLE TOASTED CHEESE CANAPES

Have soft American cheese at room temperature. Spread 1 teaspoon on each toasted canapé base. Broil until cheese is bubbly.

SAUTEED SANDWICH BITS

Use nippy spreads and make simple sandwiches. Cut into 1-inch squares. Sauté in butter.

HOT WAFFLED TEASERS

Place a very thin slice of Swiss cheese or ham or both between thinly sliced buttered bread. Spread lightly with horseradish mustard. Make sandwiches very small. Toast in waffle iron.

SIMPLE CHEESE DREAMS

Put a slice of American cheese between 2 thin slices of bread. Cut into small triangles. Broil under a moderate flame to toast both sides.

OPEN-FACED CHEESE DREAMS

Beat 2 egg whites with ⅛ teaspoon salt until very stiff. Fold in 1 cup grated American cheese seasoned with 1 teaspoon Worcestershire sauce. Toast small rounds or squares of bread on one side. Spread untoasted side with cheese-egg mixture. Top with a tiny piece of bacon. Broil under moderate flame until cheese is lightly browned and puffed.

ROQUEFORT PUFFS

Beat 1 egg white until stiff. Cream 2 ounces Roquefort cheese spread and fold into egg white. Heap on crackers or bread rounds. Bake in slow oven (300° F.) until browned (about 15 minutes). Garnish with paprika. Yield: eight 2-inch puffs.

POTATO CHIPS AU GRATIN

Sprinkle potato chips with grated American cheese. Broil only enough to melt cheese.

CHEESED TUNA FISH CANAPES

Mix flaked tuna fish with mayonnaise. Add chopped stuffed olives. Season with Worcestershire sauce. Spread on toast rounds. Sprinkle with grated cheese Broil only until cheese melts. Serve hot.

CHEESED BOLOGNA CUPS

Spread thin slices of bologna with a nippy cheese spread. Place in moderate oven (350° F.) until cheese melts and edges of bologna curl to form cups.

CHEESED SQUARES

Cut white bread into 1-inch squares. Dip in mixture of 1 beaten egg and 2 tablespoons melted butter. Roll in finely grated dry American cheese. Bake on a cooky sheet in moderate over (350° F.) until cheese melts and squares are brown.

CHEESED OYSTER CANAPES

Toast rounds of bread on one side. Spread untoasted side with Anchovy Butter. Cook oysters in white wine until edges curl, about 1 minute. Place an oyster on each round. Cover with Roquefort cheese which has been creamed with sweet butter and seasoned with pepper. Sprinkle with paprika. Broil until bubbly and lightly browned.

HOT CHEESED MUSHROOM HORS D'OEUVRES

Fill cavities of fresh mushroom caps with small pieces of sharp cheddar cheese. Dot with butter. Broil slowly until cheese melts and mushrooms are cooked through. Spear each with a cocktail pick. Serve at once.

HOT CHEESED MUSHROOM CANAPES

1 cup sliced fresh mushrooms or ½ cup sliced canned mushrooms
2 tablespoons minced onion
½ cup butter or margarine
2 tablespoons minced parsley
4 hard-cooked eggs, finely chopped
Salt and pepper
1 slightly beaten egg
Canapé bases toasted on 1 side
Grated cheese

Sauté mushrooms and onion in melted butter or margarine. Add hard-cooked eggs, parsley, and salt and pepper to taste. Add beaten egg and cook only until thick. Spread on untoasted sides of canapé bases. Sprinkle with grated cheese. Broil until cheese melts. Serve hot.

CANADIAN BACON-CHEESE GRILLS

Have Canadian bacon cut into slices ⅛ inch thick. Cut the slices into quarters. Place ½ teaspoon softened American cheese in the center of each small cracker. Cover with a quarter slice of Canadian bacon. Broil until bacon is hot and crisp at edges.

HOT CHEESE-BACON CANAPES #1

1 egg yolk, well beaten
½ cup grated nippy cheese
1 tablespoon cream
Salt and pepper
1-inch strips of bacon

Combine egg yolk, cheese, and cream. Season to taste. Toast bread squares or rounds on one side and spread mixture on untoasted side. Top each with a bacon strip. Bake in moderate oven (350° F.) until bacon is crisp.

HOT CHEESE AND BACON CANAPES #2

2 cups grated cheese
¼ cup crisp minced bacon
1 tablespoon Worcestershire sauce
Few grains cayenne
Toasted canapé bases

Mix cheese with bacon, Worcestershire sauce, and cayenne. Spread untoasted side of canapé bases. Broil under moderate heat until cheese melts.

HOT HAM AND CHEESE CANAPES #1

Cover toasted canapé bases with baked ham slices cut to same size and shape as canapé bases. Dot with bits of pimiento and chopped olive or pickle. Sprinkle heavily with grated Swiss cheese. Broil under moderate heat until cheese melts.

HOT HAM AND CHEESE CANAPES #2

Spread small toast bases with Garlic Butter. Cover with a thin slice of ham, then with a thin slice of cheese. Place on baking sheet. Bake until cheese melts. Sprinkle with paprika. Serve hot.

HOT CREAM CHEESE ROLLS

Trim crusts from unsliced loaf of bread with a very sharp knife. Cut into extremely thin slices. If necessary, flatten slices with rolling pin. Spread with softened butter, then with cream cheese. Roll up and place on baking sheet with open end at bottom. Toast under moderate broiler heat until delicately browned. Serve hot.

Variations: Snappy cheese spreads or other fillings may be substituted for cream cheese.

BACON AND CHEESE ROLLS

Place thin slices of cheese on thin slices of bread. Roll up and wrap in bacon strips. Broil slowly until bacon is done.

PICKLE-CHEESE CANAPES

Top untoasted sides of canapé rounds with slices of pickle. Sprinkle liberally with grated cheese. Bake in moderate oven (350° F.) until cheese melts.

BUBBLY CHEESED CANAPES #1

Mix softened butter or margarine with seasoned chopped crabmeat, lobster, shrimp, or hard-cooked egg. Spread on toast canapé bases. Top with grated cheese. Broil until bubbly. Serve hot.

BUBBLY CHEESED CANAPES #2

Season grated cheese with mustard or Worcestershire sauce or a little of each. Spread on toasted canapé bases or plain bread. Broil until cheese is bubbly. Serve at once.

CHEESED CRABMEAT CANAPES

Moisten crabmeat with mayonnaise. Spread on untoasted side of bread bases. Cover thickly with grated cheese. Broil under moderate heat until cheese melts.

SAVORY CHEESE CANAPES

Spread toast fingers or squares with Mustard Butter. Spread with a mixture of equal parts of minced parsley and finely chopped olives. Top each with a thin slice of American cheese. Broil under moderate heat until cheese melts. Sprinkle with paprika and serve hot.

HOT ASPARAGUS TIP CANAPES

Heat tiny canned asparagus tips in melted butter until hot throughout. Place on toast fingers. Sprinkle heavily with grated American cheese. Broil under moderate heat until cheese melts.

INDIAN CANAPES

Spread toasted or sautéed rounds of bread with a mixture of equal parts of chutney sauce and boiled ham put through the food chopper, or deviled ham. Sprinkle with grated Parmesan cheese or other well-flavored cheese. Brown in a hot oven (400° F.). Serve hot or cold garnished with parsley.

CHEESEWICH

Cut day-old bread in ¼-inch slices. Slice American cheese thin. Make sandwiches, seasoning with salt, paprika, and a light covering of prepared English mustard. Press sandwiches gently together and trim off crusts. Cut sandwiches in quarters or triangle shape. Melt some butter in frying pan. Over very low heat fry sandwiches until lightly browned, taking care in turning them that they do not separate. Serve hot.

HOT CHEESE-ONION CANAPES

Use double quantity of the Plain Pastry recipe. Roll out into thin sheet and cut strips 4 inches long and ½ inch wide. Sprinkle with ½ cup grated cheese, ½ cup chopped onion, and salt and pepper to taste. Roll as for jelly roll and fasten with toothpicks. Place on baking sheet, cut side down. Bake in very hot oven (450° F.) 15 minutes, or until done.

PIMIENTO-CHEESE CANAPE

6 *large canned pimientos*
Salt and pepper
Cayenne

¼ *pound sliced sharp American cheese*
Flour
Buttered toast rounds

Sprinkle inner surface of pimientos with salt, pepper, and cayenne to taste. Cut the cheese slices into rectangles the same size as the pimientos. Place cheese rectangles on pimientos and roll up. Skewer with toothpicks and roll in flour. Sauté in hot butter for 3 minutes, or until the cheese melts. Serve hot on the toast rounds.

HOT CHEESE BALLS #1

2 *teaspoons flour*
Dash of paprika
½ *teaspoon salt*
1 *cup grated American cheese*

2 *teaspoons minced pimiento*
1 *egg white, beaten*
¼ *cup crushed salted peanuts*

Mix flour, paprika, and salt with grated cheese. Add pimiento. Fold into egg white, beaten until stiff, but not dry. Form into small balls and roll in peanuts. Fry in deep hot fat (375° F.) until lightly browned. Serve hot.

61

HOT CHEESE BALLS #2

1½ cups grated cheese
1 tablespoon flour
¼ teaspoon salt

Few grains cayenne
3 egg whites, stiffly beaten
¾ cup fine cracker crumbs

Mix cheese, flour, salt, and cayenne. Add to stiffly beaten egg whites. Chill in refrigerator until hard. Form into small balls. Roll in crumbs and fry in deep fat (370° F.) until browned. Drain on absorbent paper. Serve hot on picks.

HOT CHEESE BALLS #3

1 pound American cheese
½ teaspoon dry mustard
Dash of Tabasco sauce
¼ teaspoon salt
2 teaspoons Worcestershire sauce

1 tablespoon flour
4 egg whites
1 tablespoon water
Dry breadcrumbs

Put cheese through meat grinder, then mash with a spoon to form a paste. Add seasonings and flour, and last, 3 stiffly beaten egg whites. Form into ½-inch balls. Chill thoroughly. Just before cooking, roll in breadcrumbs, then in remaining egg white which has been beaten and mixed with water. Fry in deep fat (375° F.) until golden brown. Drain on absorbent paper. Serve hot on picks.

BAKED HOT CHEESE BALLS #4

2 cups grated sharp cheddar cheese
½ cup butter
1 cup flour

⅛ teaspoon salt
¼ teaspoon paprika
¼ teaspoon dry mustard

Blend cheese and butter. Add flour, salt, paprika, and mustard. Form into tiny balls. Place on greased baking sheet. Bake in moderate oven (350° F.) about 10 minutes.

COTTAGE CHEESE BALLS

Mix 1½ pounds cottage cheese, 4 tablespoons melted butter, 4 tablespoons caraway seed, 1 egg, and 1 tablespoon sugar. Blend thoroughly. Form into small balls. Place on baking sheet. Bake in moderate oven (350° F.) 12 to 15 minutes. Serve hot on picks.

TURKISH CHEESE APPETIZERS (BEUREKS)

Cut ½ pound Gruyère cheese into small pieces. Put into a saucepan with ¼ cup thick white sauce. Stir until cheese is melted and mixture is thick. Spread on a platter to cool. Chill if necessary. Shape into small sausage-like shapes. Wrap each in a thin piece of plain pastry and fry in deep hot fat (385° F.) until golden brown. Drain. Serve hot or cold.

ARMENIAN CHEESE BOURAG

2 cups sifted all-purpose flour
¼ teaspoon salt
3 teaspoons baking powder
3 tablespoons butter
½ cup milk (about)
½ pound sharp cheese, grated
3 tablespoons minced parsley
¼ teaspoon salt

Mix and sift flour, salt, and baking powder. Cut in butter with a pastry blender or 2 knives and mix to a dough with milk. Roll out very thin on a floured board and cut into 2-inch squares. Mix remaining ingredients together. Put squares together by pairs with tablespoon of cheese mixture between. Press edges well together and fry until brown in deep hot fat (360° to 370° F.). Drain and serve.

HOT CHEESE AND CLAM CANAPES

3-ounce package cream cheese
1 small can minced clams
Toasted canapé bases
Salt and pepper

Use bread cut ½ inch thick and toasted on one side. Drain clams and mix with cream cheese, adding salt and pepper to taste. Spread on untoasted side of canapé bases. Broil until delicately browned. Yield: about 12 canapés.

HOT TOMATO AND ANCHOVY CANAPES

2 tablespoons butter
2 tablespoons anchovy paste
8 toast rounds
8 tomato slices
3 tablespoons grated American cheese

Mix butter and anchovy paste. Spread on toast rounds. Place a thin slice of tomato on top of each. Sprinkle with grated cheese. Place under moderate broiler until cheese is melted. Serve at once very hot, garnished with chopped parsley.

HOT CHEESED SARDINE CANAPES

Rub mixing bowl with a cut clove of garlic. Mash sardines to a paste, seasoning with lemon juice and prepared mustard. Spread on toasted rye bread rounds. Sprinkle lightly with grated cheese. Brown in hot oven (400° F.).

FRANKFURTER-CHEESE-BACON HORS D'OEUVRES

Slit frankfurters in half lengthwise. Fill each sandwich-fashion with a ¼-inch stick of sharp cheese. Secure with toothpicks placed at ¾-inch intervals along frankfurters. Slice between picks to make bite-size servings. Wrap each with a piece of bacon. Secure with toothpick. Broil until bacon is crisp. Serve hot.

WELSH RABBIT CANAPES

1 *cup freshly grated American cheese*
½ *cup finely chopped ham*
2 *tablespoons light cream*
1 *teaspoon prepared mustard*

Dash of cayenne
¼ *teaspoon Worcestershire sauce*
Toasted bread bases
Grated American cheese

Combine cheese, ham, cream, and seasonings. Heat in top of double boiler until cheese melts. Spread warm mixture on bases. Sprinkle with grated cheese. Broil lightly. Serve hot.

FRANK TOP-NOTCHERS

Slit franks lengthwise down the middle without cutting all the way through. Insert a stick of cheese. Cut into 1-inch pieces and wrap each piece in bacon. A pick holds all in place. Broil to heat and crisp the bacon. Keep hot on a grill or in pan set over hot water.

Frank Top-Notchers

Hot Fish and Seafood Canapes

and Hors d'oeuvres

In the chapter on the Dunking Trays a suggestion was made that shrimp, fried, boiled, or canned, as well as chunks of lobster and crabmeat should be speared on picks for "dunking." In this section along with other canapés and hors d'oeuvres you'll find recipes for other fish and seafood that may be used in this manner.

HOT CRABMEAT CANAPES

12 ounces crabmeat
Salt and pepper
3 tablespoons butter
1 small onion, minced fine
2 tablespoons flour

1 cup broth or water
2 ounces grated Parmesan cheese
2 ounces grated Swiss cheese
Toast squares

Season crabmeat with salt and pepper to taste. Melt 2 tablespoons butter in a saucepan. Add onion and sauté gently until cooked. Add 1 tablespoon flour and stir constantly for 2 minutes. Add broth or water and crabmeat and let cook slowly 15 minutes, stirring occasionally. Turn mixture into a bowl and let cool. Place 1 tablespoon butter in a pan and blend in 1 tablespoon flour; add the cheese, mix well and turn out to cool. Spread the toast squares with the crabmeat mixture. Roll the cheese into tiny balls and place one in the center of each canapé. Place under broiler until lightly browned, about 5 minutes.

SEA DEVIL

Combine crabmeat with a thick cream sauce. Season with salt, pepper, and a little curry powder. Spread on small pieces of toast. Sprinkle with grated cheese. Dot with butter. Put under broiler to toast lightly. Serve very hot.

HOT LOBSTER CANAPES

½ *pound cooked or canned lobster meat, chopped*
1 *cup medium white sauce*
½ *pound mushrooms, sliced and sautéed*
1 *tablespoon minced green pepper*
1 *tablespoon chopped pimiento*

1 *teaspoon Worcestershire sauce*
2 *tablespoons sherry wine*
½ *teaspoon salt (about)*
20 *small toast diamonds or rounds*
½ *cup grated American or Swiss cheese*
3 *tablespoons butter*

Mix lobster, white sauce, mushrooms, pepper, pimiento, Worcestershire sauce, and sherry. Add salt to taste. Heat and pile on toast. Sprinkle with cheese and bits of butter. Broil under moderate heat until cheese is bubbly. Yield: 20 canapés.

Variations: Substitute cooked or canned crabmeat or shrimp for lobster.

HOT LOBSTER AND BACON CANAPES

Use canned or freshly cooked lobster meat. Season with salt and paprika. Brown in melted butter in which a little minced onion is cooked. Roll when brown in slices of uncooked bacon. Fasten with toothpicks. Broil until bacon is crisp. Serve on toast squares or rounds with coating of tartar sauce. Garnish with pimiento strips.

FRIED OYSTERS OR SCALLOPS

Drain oysters or scallops. Dry carefully between towels. Roll in flour seasoned with salt and pepper, then in beaten egg diluted with 1 tablespoon water. Roll in dry bread or cracker crumbs. Fry in deep fat (375° F.) until golden brown. Drain on absorbent paper. Serve on hot toast rounds spread with tartar sauce.

SCALLOPS ON HORSEBACK

1 *pound scallops*
3 *tablespoons butter*
8 *slices of bacon*

1 *green pepper*
Salt and pepper
1 *large raw potato*

Place scallops in a saucepan with the butter and cook for 5 minutes. Cut bacon into 2-inch pieces. Cut pepper into 1-inch squares. Arrange bacon, scallops, and green pepper alternately on toothpicks. Sprinkle scallops with salt and pepper. Stick the toothpicks upright into a large raw potato. Bake in hot oven (400° F.) 20 minutes, or until bacon is crisp and scallops are browned.

SAUTEED SCALLOPS

1 pound scallops
¼ cup butter or margarine
¼ cup flour

¼ teaspoon salt
⅛ teaspoon pepper

Wipe scallops with a damp paper towel. Roll in flour seasoned with salt and pepper. Melt butter in skillet. Add scallops and cook only 5 minutes over high flame, turning constantly to brown evenly. Serve at once on picks. If large sea scallops are used, cut in small pieces.

BOILED FRESH SHRIMP

To 1 quart boiling water, add 1 tablespoon white vinegar, 1 teaspoon salt, dash of pepper, 1 bay leaf, 1 whole onion, and 1 whole carrot. Cook 10 minutes. Drop in shrimp. Lower heat and simmer 5 minutes until shrimp are pink and tender. Let shrimp cool in cooking water, then drain and peel.

Note: In preparing all shrimp, fresh, boiled, or canned, the black vein along the back is removed with a sharply pointed knife, then the shrimp are rinsed under cold water.

FRIED SHRIMP FOR HORS D'OEUVRES

1 pound raw shrimp, peeled and cleaned
1 well beaten egg
1 teaspoon salt
About ¼ teaspoon black pepper

1 teaspoon chopped parsley
1 tablespoon prepared mustard
1 teaspoon dried basil
1 mashed clove garlic
1 teaspoon chopped chives

Mix shrimp with other ingredients. Let stand overnight. Sauté in butter or fry in deep fat (365° F.). Serve hot on picks.

HOT SHRIMP HORS D'OEUVRES

Melt ¼ cup butter in a heavy skillet. Add 6 tablespoons lemon juice. When mixture bubbles add 3 pounds cooked, cleaned shrimp. Keep hot on very low heat. Serve with Standard Cocktail Sauce #1 as a dunk.

HOT SHRIMP CANAPES

Wrap cleaned, cooked or canned shrimp in small slices of bacon. Fasten with picks. Brown slowly in frying pan, or grill in the broiler, or bake in hot oven (400° F.) until bacon is done. Replace burnt picks with fresh ones.

67

Clams Casino

CLAMS CASINO

Open clams carefully to retain juice. Remove upper shell, leaving clams in deeper half. Sprinkle each with few drops of lemon juice, a bit of finely minced green pepper, and chopped onion. Season with salt and pepper. Put 3 bits of bacon on each. Set in pan and bake in very hot oven (450° F.) or under broiler until bacon crisps.

FRIED CLAM CAKES

2 *cups sifted flour*	1 *cup milk*
1 *teaspoon baking powder*	½ *cup clam liquor*
½ *teaspoon salt*	1 *pint fresh clams*
2 *eggs, well beaten*	*Deep fat for frying*

Mix and sift flour, baking powder, and salt. Add well beaten eggs, milk and clam liquor slowly; stir well and add clams which have been ground quite fine in a food chopper. Drop by spoonfuls into deep fat (375° F.). When nicely browned, remove from kettle and drain. Serve hot.

COCKTAIL FISH BALLS #1

1 *cup salt codfish*	½ *tablespoon butter*
2½ *cups potatoes*	⅛ *teaspoon pepper*
1 *egg, well beaten*	

Wash fish in cold water. Pick in very small pieces or cut, using scissors. Wash, pare, and soak potatoes, cutting in pieces of uniform size before

68

measuring. Cook fish and potatoes in boiling water to cover until potatoes are nearly soft. Drain thoroughly through strainer and return to kettle in which they were cooked. Shake over heat until thoroughly dry. Mash thoroughly and add butter, egg, and pepper. Beat with fork 2 minutes. Add salt if necessary. Take up by spoonfuls and sauté in butter or fry 1 minute in deep fat (385° F.) until brown. Drain on paper. Serve hot with toothpicks.

COCKTAIL FISH BALLS #2

Shape canned codfish cake mixture into small balls or cones the size of marbles and roll in flour. Fry in deep fat (375° F.) until brown. Insert cocktail pick and serve hot on hors d'oeuvres tray with ketchup.

HOT OYSTER BALLS

1 *pint oysters*	*Dash of Tabasco or cayenne*
1 *teaspoon grated onion*	*Pinch of mace*
1 *teaspoon minced parsley*	2 *eggs*
1 *cup soft breadcrumbs*	2 *tablespoons butter*
About ¼ *teaspoon salt*	*Corn meal or fine dry bread-*
About ¼ *teaspoon pepper*	*crumbs*

Pour boiling water over drained oysters. Drain well and chop fine. Add onion, parsley, and soft breadcrumbs. Season to taste and mix to stiff paste with 1 beaten egg and the butter. Form into small balls. Roll in beaten egg, then in corn meal or dry crumbs. Fry in deep fat (360° F.) until browned. Drain on absorbent paper. Serve hot on picks.

BROILED BREADED OYSTERS

Roll fresh oysters in mixture of half bread and half cracker crumbs. Press flat with hands. Broil 2 minutes on each side. Salt lightly and brush with melted butter. Serve on buttered hot toast rounds.

ANGELS ON HORSEBACK

Wrap small oysters in 3-inch strips of bacon. Fasten with picks. Broil in oven until bacon is crisp. Remove picks and place on ovals of toasted bread spread with tartar sauce.

HOT OYSTER CANAPES #1

Place small oysters on small rounds of toast. Sprinkle with salt, pepper, and lemon juice, then with grated cheese. If desired, add a tiny piece of bacon. Broil just until cheese melts. Serve immediately.

HOT OYSTER CANAPES #2

36 oysters
2 tablespoons Hollandaise sauce
Buttered toast squares

2 tablespoons minced parsley
2 tablespoons butter

Blanch oysters and chop very fine. Mix with sauce and spread over buttered toast squares. Sprinkle with parsley. Dot with butter. Broil under moderate heat for a few minutes. Serve very hot.

HOT OYSTER AND MUSHROOM CANAPES

Peel large mushrooms and remove stems. Dip in melted butter or olive oil. Put a fresh oyster in each. Season to taste with salt, pepper, paprika, and celery salt, if desired. Broil under moderate heat. Serve on hot toasted canapé bases or in the oyster shells.

DEVILED ROE CANAPES

Mix 1 tablespoon melted butter, ⅓ teaspoon mustard, 1¼ teaspoons Worcester sauce, and salt to taste. Drain 4 pieces canned fish roe and roll in this mixture. Mash the roe and spread on toast squares. Place in hot oven (425° F.) for 5 minutes. Serve with lemon wedges.

BACON WITH SHAD ROE

Wrap small wedges of canned shad roe in small pieces of bacon. Fry until crisp. Spear each with a pick.

HOT TUNA CANAPES

Combine 1 can (6 to 7 ounces) drained, flaked tuna with ¼ cup mayonnaise and 1 tablespoon each ketchup and vinegar. Add salt, cayenne, and Worcestershire sauce to taste. Pile on toast bases or crackers. Broil under moderate heat. Garnish with chopped parsley, pimiento, or green pepper. Serve hot.

TOASTED SARDINE ROLLS

Drain oil from sardines, mash and mix with horseradish and lemon juice to taste. Spread on thin squares of very fresh bread. Roll up. Fasten with toothpicks. Brush with melted butter. Toast in hot oven (400° F.) until delicately browned. Serve at once.

PARMESAN-SARDINE CANAPES

Drain and bone skinless sardines. Mash and season with finely minced celery, ketchup, minced onion, and pepper. Add enough mayonnaise to make a paste of spreading consistency. Spread lightly on thin slices of ice-box rye bread. Sprinkle with Parmesan cheese. Broil until well heated throughout.

WHOLE BROILED SARDINE CANAPES

Mix 2 tablespoons soft butter with 1 teaspoon dry mustard and a few drops Worcestershire sauce. Drain large sardines and brush with mixture. Dip in cracker crumbs. Broil quickly. Serve on toast strips and sprinkle with lemon juice. Garnish with minced parsley .

Biscuit and Pastry Hors d'oeuvres

ALMOST all of the hors d'oeuvres that follow lend themselves to infinite variations in fillings. As a starter we suggest that you try the Cornish Pasties or Piroshke à la Russe with a nicely seasoned meat filling—but make lots of them. You'll find all other canapés and hors d'oeuvres practically ignored until these are "all gone."

CORNISH PASTIES

¼ pound mutton or beef, diced
3 small potatoes, peeled and diced
1 small onion, minced
Salt and pepper

2 cups sifted all-purpose flour
1 teaspoon baking powder
6 tablespoons shortening
Cold water

Mix meat, potatoes, and onion. Season to taste with salt and pepper. Mix and sift flour, baking powder, and a dash of salt. Rub in shortening. Add enough cold water to make a stiff dough. Roll out on floured board in a square about ⅛ inch thick. Cut into small squares. Place a spoonful of mixture on each. Wet edges with cold water. Draw opposite edges together and press well together with thumb and finger to seal in filling. Place on greased pan. Bake in hot oven (400° F.) until browned, about 30 minutes. Serve hot.

PIROSHKE A LA RUSSE

1½ cups sifted all-purpose flour
¼ teaspoon baking powder
½ teaspoon salt
¼ teaspoon pepper

½ cup shortening
1 egg
¼ cup cold water (about)

Mix and sift dry ingredients. Cut in shortening. Add egg and gradually add enough water to keep dough together. Roll out on a floured board to ⅛-inch thickness. Cut into 3-inch rounds or squares. Place a spoonful of filling in center of each. Pinch edges together well to seal in filling. Brush with melted shortening or egg yolk diluted with equal amount of water. They will form triangles from squares and half-moons from rounds. Bake in moderate oven (375° F.) on greased pans for 20 minutes or until brown. Serve hot.

Variations: Piroshke may be made in any desired size from yeast dough, well kneaded, or any pie crust dough. If yeast dough is used be sure to let them rise for 1 to 1½ hours after they have been filled.

PIROSHKE FILLINGS

Meat Filling: Brown 1 minced onion in hot fat or salad oil. Add 1 pound lean ground beef or veal. Season to taste. Brown slightly.

Rice and Mushroom Filling: Brown 1 minced onion in hot fat or salad oil. Add ½ cup chopped canned or fresh mushrooms or ¼ cup chopped dried mushrooms which have been soaked in cold salted water. Add 1 cup cooked rice and season to taste. Mix thoroughly.

Beef and Onion Filling: Fry 1 pound chopped lean beef and 2 sliced onions lightly in hot fat. Remove and add 3 hard-cooked eggs, 1 teaspoon fennel or dill, salt and pepper to taste. Mix well.

Other Fillings: Use highly seasoned chopped cooked liver, poultry, or fish and seafood fillings. Cooked buckwheat groats and highly seasoned chopped cooked lung are popular with people of Eastern European origin.

HOT TASTY TURNOVERS

Prepare Plain Pastry and roll out on a floured board to ⅛-inch thickness. Cut into small rounds or squares and fill with seasoned meat or fish fillings. Fold over to form half moons from the rounds or triangles from the squares. Prick the top of pastry to allow escape of steam. Brush with milk. Place on ungreased baking sheet. Store in refrigerator until ready to use. Bake in very hot oven (450° F.) 15 to 20 minutes. Serve immediately.

LIVER SAUSAGE TURNOVERS

Plain Pastry	½ teaspoon grated onion
3 ounces liver sausage	¾ teaspoon mustard
1½ teaspoons prepared horse-radish	

Blend all ingredients together. Cut rolled pastry dough into 2-inch squares. On each square place 1 teaspoon sausage mixture. Fold over to form triangles. Press edges together with fork. Prick top of pastry to allow escape of steam. Brush with milk. Place on ungreased baking sheet. Store in refrigerator until ready to use. Bake in very hot oven (450° F.) 15 to 20 minutes. Serve immediately. Yield: about 24.

SARDINE SURPRISES

Prepare Plain Pastry and roll pastry thin. Cut into squares the length of sardines. Cut each square diagonally to form triangles. Have small sardines drained on absorbent paper. Lay a sardine on each piece of pastry. Sprinkle with lemon juice. Fold point of triangle opposite diagonal over sardine. Press tightly to opposite side. Place on ungreased baking street. Store in refrigerator until ready to use. Bake in very hot oven (450° F.) 15 to 20 minutes. Yield: about 24.

OLIVE PASTRY SNACKS

Prepare Plain Pastry. Roll out ⅛ inch thick on a slightly floured board. Cut into 2-inch squares. Place a medium-sized stuffed olive in each square and fold pastry around it. Roll lightly between the palms of hands to form balls. Bake on ungreased cooky sheet in very hot oven (450° F.) until crisp and delicately browned, about 15 minutes. These snacks may be prepared in advance and kept in refrigerator until ready to be baked.

PIGS IN A BLANKET

Prepare Plain Pastry. Roll out ⅛ inch thick on a slightly floured board. Cut into small squares. Roll a small cocktail sausage in each square. Bake in very hot oven (450° F.) until pastry is nicely browned, about 15 minutes. Serve hot.

Biscuit Teasers

BISCUIT TEASERS

Prepare the recipe for Baking Powder Biscuits, increasing salt to 1 teaspoon and using only enough milk to form a soft dough. Roll out to ¼-inch thickness. Cut into rounds about 1 inch in diameter with a small biscuit cutter. Slice tiny cocktail sausages or other highly seasoned sausages very thin. Cover a biscuit with sausage slices, then with another biscuit, more sausage and another biscuit. Press together at one side. Set "sandwiches" on end in small muffin pans. Bake in very hot oven (450° F.) 12 to 15 minutes. Serve hot.

TINY FILLED BISCUITS

Prepare the Baking Powder Biscuit recipe. Make tiny hot baking powder biscuits. Split and spread half with a favorite cheese spread, with deviled ham and pickle relish, minced sautéed mushrooms, finely chopped chicken and olive spread, or a favorite seafood spread. Cover with other half. Serve hot.

Waffled Wafers

WAFFLED WAFERS

Prepare the recipe for Baking Powder Biscuits. Cut into 2-inch rounds. Cover half the biscuits with a sandwich spread and cover each with another biscuit. Place a "sandwich" in each section of a hot waffle iron. Bake until well browned, about 3½ minutes. Serve hot.

QUICKIE MEAT ROLLS

Use a prepared biscuit mix or prepare the recipe for Baking Powder Biscuits. Roll dough out thin. Spread with liverwurst. Roll up jelly-roll fashion, or wrap Vienna sausage halves in the thinly rolled dough, letting the edges show. Bake in very hot oven (450° F.) about 10 minutes.

QUICK FRANKS IN BLANKET

Use a prepared biscuit mix or prepare the recipe for Baking Powder Biscuits. Roll dough out ⅜ inch thick. Cut into small rectangles to fit cocktail frankfurters. Place a frankfurter on each alternate rectangle. Wet the edges of the dough and cover each frank with a biscuit rectangle. Pinch edges together to seal. Place on baking sheet and bake in very hot oven (450° F.) 10 to 12 minutes.

SAUSAGE ROLLS

Form finely ground sausage meat into a long thin roll. Wrap in Plain Pastry. Cut into ¾-inch slices. Place on baking sheet. Bake in very hot oven (450° F.) until crisp and delicately browned. Serve hot.

BISCUIT SANDWICHES

⅔ cup sifted all-purpose flour
½ teaspoon salt
6 tablespoons grated American cheese

2 tablespoons butter
2 to 3 tablespoons milk
Deviled ham

Mix and sift flour with salt. Cut or rub in the cheese and butter. Add milk to form dough. Roll out ⅛ inch thick. Cut into tiny rounds. Spread deviled ham on alternate rounds. Cover with unspread rounds. Pinch edges together. Bake in very hot oven (450° F.) 12 to 15 minutes. For variety, you may want to try other favorite fillings in place of deviled ham.

BEEF BITES

⅓ cup mayonnaise
1 cup sifted all-purpose flour

1 tablespoon cold water
½ pound lean ground meat, seasoned to taste

Add mayonnaise to flour and stir with a fork. Add water and stir until dough begins to form. Roll out to long strip about 4 inches wide and ¼ inch thick. Press the seasoned meat into a rope shape and place on top of rolled dough. Moisten edge of dough and bring together around meat. Cut in 1-inch slices. Bake in very hot oven (450° F.) 15 to 20 minutes. Serve hot or cold.

ANCHOVY TURNOVERS

3-ounce package cream cheese
½ cup butter or margarine

1 cup sifted all-purpose flour
Anchovy paste

Blend cheese and butter. Mix with flour. Chill. Roll very thin and cut with 2-inch cooky cutter. Spread with anchovy paste. Fold over and bake in hot oven (400° F.) 10 minutes. Serve hot. Yield: about 48.

TINY SAUSAGE RISSOULES

Make Puff Paste and roll out ⅛-inch thick. Cut into rounds. Place a tiny cooked sausage in center. Fold pastry over. Press edges together with tines of fork or a pastry marker. Prick top. Brush tops lightly with a mixture of 1 egg yolk beaten with 1 teaspoon cold water. Bake in very hot oven (450° F.) 10 minutes. To vary, substitute small sardines or rolled anchovy fillets for sausage. Serve hot.

HUSH PUPPIES

2 cups corn meal
1 tablespoon flour
1 teaspoon baking powder
½ teaspoon baking soda
1 teaspoon salt

3 tablespoons finely chopped onions
1 egg, well beaten
1 cup buttermilk

Mix and sift dry ingredients. Add onion, well beaten egg, and buttermilk. Drop by the spoonful into hot fat. Fry until golden brown. Drain on absorbent paper.

PASTRY SNAILS

Prepare Plain Pastry. Roll into very thin oblongs. Spread with any of the fillings given below. Roll up jelly-roll fashion and cut into ½-inch slices. Place on greased cooky sheet. Bake in hot oven (425° F.) until crisp and delicately browned, 10 to 15 minutes.

FILLINGS FOR PASTRY SNAILS

Deviled Ham: Spread with deviled ham. Season with mustard and salt. Sprinkle with grated cheese, then with a little paprika.

Cream Cheese: Soften cream cheese with just a little cream. Season with salt and paprika.

American Cheese: Spread with grated American cheese seasoned to taste.

Roquefort Cheese: Crumble Roquefort or blue cheese and blend with equal amount cream cheese which has been softened with just a bit of cream.

Cottage Cheese: Season cottage cheese with salt and pepper to taste and a little paprika, if desired.

Anchovy-Cheese: Soften cream cheese and blend with equal amount of anchovy paste or anchovy fillets mashed to a paste.

Other Fillings: You may want to experiment with many of the fillings suggested for canapé spreads such as the cheese, fish, and seafood fillings.

KNISHES

2 cups sifted all-purpose flour
1 teaspoon baking powder
½ teaspoon salt

2 tablespoons water
1 tablespoon vegetable oil
2 eggs, well beaten

Mix and sift flour, baking powder, and salt. Form a well in center and add water, oil, and eggs. Mix and form into a smooth dough. Roll out

77

on a lightly floured board to ⅛-inch thickness. Cut into rounds or squares or if desired leave whole. Fill with desired filling. Moisten edges and fold over the filling. Press edges firmly together. Bake in a pan greased with hot vegetable oil in a moderate oven (350° F.) until brown and crisp. If the dough is left in a whole sheet, fill and roll up like a jelly roll. The fillings given here are only suggestions. In fact the methods for making knishes and the fillings are limited only by the imagination of the cook.

CHICKEN FILLING FOR KNISHES

2 *cups chopped cooked chicken*
½ *cup breadcrumbs*

About 1 *cup chicken gravy*
Salt and pepper

Combine all ingredients. Season to taste.

MEAT FILLING FOR KNISHES

2 *cups cooked ground meat*
½ *cup mashed potatoes*
2 *tablespoons melted fat*
1 *small onion, minced*

½ *teaspoon salt*
¼ *teaspoon pepper*
1 *egg, beaten*
Paprika (optional)

Combine all ingredients. Mix well.

LIVER FILLING FOR KNISHES

1 *onion, minced*
1 *tablespoon chicken fat*
½ *pound cooked liver*
¼ *pound cooked lung*
½ *pound cooked beef*

½ *cup cooked buckwheat groats*
    or rice
Salt and pepper
1 *egg*

Fry minced onion in chicken fat until lightly browned. Put liver, lung, and beef through food chopper. Combine with remaining ingredients.

CHEESE KNISHES

DOUGH:
4 *cups sifted all-purpose flour*
2 *teaspoons baking powder*
½ *teaspoon salt*
2 *eggs, well beaten*
1 *tablespoon melted butter*
1 *cup thick sour cream*

FILLING:
1 *pound dry cottage cheese*
½ *cup thick sour cream*
2 *tablespoons bread or matzo crumbs*
2 *tablespoons melted butter*
2 *tablespoons sugar*
2 *tablespoons raisins*
2 *eggs, well beaten*

78

Mix and sift flour, baking powder, and salt. Add eggs, butter, and sour cream. Knead into a soft dough, adding a little milk if necessary. Roll out on floured board to ¼-inch thickness. Cut into small rounds or squares. Fill with cheese filling made by combining the ingredients in the order given. Moisten edges; fold over and pinch edges firmly together. Place in a greased baking pan. Bake in moderate oven (350° F.) until brown on top.

Miscellaneous Hot Canapes
and Hors d'oeuvres

CHICKEN LIVER-WATER CHESTNUT
HORS D'OEUVRES #1

Slice canned water chestnuts in 3 parts. Cut chicken livers into slices slightly larger than chestnut slices. Make sandwiches of 2 slices of liver and 1 slice of chestnut. Wrap each in bacon strips. Secure with toothpicks. Fry in deep hot fat.

CHICKEN LIVER-WATER CHESTNUT
HORS D'OEUVRES #2

Half-cook strips of bacon. Cut chicken livers in quarters and sauté in butter for 1 minute. Season with salt and pepper. Put each quarter of liver on a slice of water chestnut. Wrap each with a half-cooked bacon slice. Fasten with toothpicks. Broil until bacon is crisp. Serve hot.

BAKED CHICKEN LIVERS #1

Rinse chicken livers in cold water. Cut each in half. Spread with a mixture of equal parts finely chopped olives and prepared mustard. Wrap each piece in a small slice of bacon. Fasten with picks. Roll in fine breadcrumbs. Bake in hot oven (400° F.) 10 to 15 minutes. Serve hot.

BAKED CHICKEN LIVERS #2

Half-cook bacon strips. Cut chicken livers in halves and sauté in butter for 1 minute. Season with salt and pepper and a little minced onion. Wrap with bacon strips. Bake or broil. Serve hot.

FRENCH-FRIED CHICKEN LIVERS (Chinese Style)

Cut chicken livers into small strips. Dip in soy sauce, then in a very light batter made of egg and flour. Fry in deep hot fat (270° F.).

CHICKEN BALLS

Mince 2½ cups cooked chicken. Add ½ teaspoon minced onion, ¼ teaspoon salt, and 2 tablespoons mayonnaise. Form into small balls. Roll balls in flour and dip in melted butter or margarine. Brown quickly in hot oven (400° F.). Serve hot.

PETITE HAMBURGER CANAPES

Season ½ pound lean ground beef with 1 teaspoon minced onion, ½ teaspoon salt, ⅛ teaspoon pepper, and a dash of Worcestershire sauce. Mix thoroughly. Spread on toasted canapé bases. Broil until done. Yield: about 24 (2-inch) canapés.

HOT CHILI-BEEF CANAPES

1 *pound ground beef*	¼ *cup ketchup*
1 *tablespoon chili powder*	12 *slices toast, buttered and*
1 *teaspoon salt*	*crusts cut off*
Dash of Tabasco sauce	*Chili sauce*

Stir and heat meat, chili powder, salt, Tabasco, and ketchup in skillet until red color disappears and mixture becomes spreadable. Spread on hot buttered toast. At serving time, cut toast into 8 triangles or 9 squares. Bake in very hot oven (450° F.) 10 minutes. To serve, garnish with a dash of chili sauce.

HOT CHICKEN GIBLET CANAPES

Cover squares or rounds of toast with chopped chicken giblets seasoned to taste. Sprinkle generously with grated Parmesan cheese. Broil under moderate heat until cheese melts.

HAMBURGERS IN BLANKETS

Form seasoned ground beef into small sausage-like shapes. Wrap each in a small thin slice of bacon. Broil under moderate heat until done. Serve very hot on a small canapé base with a slice of mild onion.

Tiny Meat Balls

TINY HOT MEAT BALLS #1

½ *pound ground round steak*
¼ *cup evaporated milk*
½ *teaspoon salt*

⅛ *teaspoon pepper*
1 *teaspoon Angostura bitters*
Breadcrumbs

Mix meat, milk, salt, pepper, and bitters. Roll into small balls. Coat lightly with breadcrumbs. Brown in bacon fat in a hot skillet. Drain on paper. Serve hot on picks.

TINY HOT MEAT BALLS #2

1 *pound ground round steak*
1 *cup fine dry breadcrumbs*
2 *tablespoons minced onion*
2 *tablespoons minced green pepper*

1 *teaspoon salt*
⅛ *teaspoon black pepper*
Dash of cayenne
Milk to moisten slightly
1 *egg, slightly beaten*

Combine all ingredients. Shape into tiny balls. Brown on all sides in butter. Add a little hot water, bouillon, or meat stock to balls and keep hot in chafing dish or top of double boiler while being served. Serve with picks.

FRIED RICE BALLS

Form ½-inch balls from a snappy cheese. Spread lightly with prepared mustard. Roll each ball in salted cooked rice. Use rice that sticks together rather than rice that is fluffy or steamed. Roll balls in hands to make them firm and compact. Fry in deep hot fat until lightly browned. Serve hot on picks.

Variations: Use cooked cleaned shrimp, stuffed olives, or anchovy paste balls instead of cheese.

SMALL SWEDISH MEAT BALLS

1 *pound lean beef*	¼ *teaspoon pepper*
½ *pound lean pork*	1 *clove garlic, mashed fine*
1 *pound veal*	⅛ *teaspoon nutmeg*
4 *slices bread*	⅛ *teaspoon allspice*
¾ *cup milk*	2 *eggs, slightly beaten*
1 *onion, finely chopped*	*Fat for frying*
2 *teaspoons salt*	2 *cups beef bouillon*

Have meats ground together 2 or 3 times. Crumble bread and add milk. Stir to paste-like consistency. Add to meat in a mixing bowl. Add seasonings and eggs. Mix until well blended. Form into 1 -inch balls. Set on waxed paper and let dry for half an hour. Brown meat balls in ½-inch of hot fat in heavy skillet. Place browned balls in single layer in large shallow baking pan. Add hot bouillon and bake in moderate oven (350° F.) until bouillon is absorbed, about 30 minutes. Serve hot on picks without gravy or sauce.

Variation: Remove browned balls from skillet. Pour off all but 3 tablespoons of fat. Stir in 4 tablespoons flour. Add enough water to make desired consistency of gravy. Boil 3 minutes. Put in top of double boiler. Add meat balls. Keep warm until served.

Small Swedish Meat Balls

PORK SAUSAGE BALLS #1

1 *pound pork sausage meat*
¼ *cup minced onion*
⅓ *cup water*
¼ *cup lemon juice*
2 *tablespoons vinegar*

2 *teaspoons Worcestershire*
sauce
2 *tablespoons sugar*
½ *teaspoon salt*
1 *teaspoon prepared mustard*
Dash of cayenne or Tabasco
sauce

Form sausage meat into small balls. Brown slowly on all sides. Remove balls and drain off all but 1 tablespoon fat. Brown onion lightly, stirring frequently. Add remaining ingredients. Simmer until thickened, 15 to 20 minutes. Pour sauce into a chafing dish or top of double boiler. Stick each ball with a pick and stand up in sauce.

PORK SAUSAGE BALLS #2

Shape seasoned pork sausage meat into tiny balls. Heat slowly in a skillet until balls are evenly browned and thoroughly cooked. Serve on picks with slices of stuffed olive.

SAUERKRAUT BALLS

½ *pound lean ham*
½ *pound lean pork*
½ *pound corned beef*
1 *medium-sized onion*
1 *teaspoon minced parsley*
3 *tablespoons shortening*
2 *cups flour*
1 *teaspoon salt*

1 *teaspoon dry mustard*
2 *cups milk*
2 *pounds sauerkraut, cooked and*
drained
Flour
2 *eggs, slightly beaten*
Dry breadcrumbs

Put ham, pork, corned beef, and onion through food chopper, using medium blade. Add parsley and blend well. Sauté in shortening until browned. Add flour, salt, mustard, and milk. Blend thoroughly. Cook, stirring constantly, until thick. Add sauerkraut and put entire mixture through food chopper. Mix thoroughly. Cook in skillet, stirring constantly, until thick. Cool. Form into balls the size of a walnut. Roll balls in flour. Dip in beaten egg. Roll in crumbs. Fry in deep fat (370° F.) until browned. Serve hot on picks.

HOT BRAUNSCHWEIGER CANAPES

Toast bread canapé bases on one side. Spread untoasted side with Mustard Butter. Cover thickly with mashed Braunschweiger which has been seasoned with a little grated onion. Broil under moderate heat until hot and puffy, 8 to 10 minutes. Garnish with stuffed olive slices before serving.

KIDNEY SPOON CAKES

Wash 1 pound kidney and put through food chopper. Add 1 teaspoon salt and 2 eggs; beat until well mixed. Drop into hot fat by spoonfuls. Brown thoroughly on one side. Turn and brown second side until crisp. Serve hot.

HOT NUTTY CANAPES

Cut slices of rye bread into finger-length sandwiches. Spread with prepared mustard, then with a mixture of ½ cup ground ham mixed with 1 tablespoon chili sauce and ¼ cup thinly sliced Brazil nuts. Toast and serve hot.

THREE LITTLE PIGS

Cut link pork sausage into 1-inch segments. Remove crusts from slices of bread. Cut each slice in 3 strips. Toast one side. Butter other side. Sprinkle generously with ground sage and cayenne pepper. Fry sausage segments on one side, and putting this side next to the butter, place 3 of the pieces on each strip of bread. Toast in oven and serve hot. -

FRANKFURTER ROLLS

Wrap tiny cocktail frankfurters in thin slices of white bread (crust removed). Spread with grated cheese seasoned with cayenne. Fasten with toothpicks. Place on baking sheet. Bake in hot oven (400° F.) until cheese melts.

TINY STUFFED FRANKFURTERS

Cut small crosswise slits in cocktail-size frankfurters and spread mustard in the slits. Insert tiny slices of onion. Broil under moderate heat turning to brown on all sides. Baste with a savory butter while broiling. Serve hot.

VIENNA PICKUPS

Trim crusts from slices of bread. Roll the bread around Vienna sausage. Seal the edges with mayonnaise. Fasten with pick. Bake or broil until lightly brown.

BACON PINWHEELS

Trim the crusts from a fresh loaf of white bread and cut ¼-inch lengthwise slices. Spread each slice with cream cheese which has softened at room temperature. Roll up each slice like a jelly roll. Cut each roll in half crosswise, and wrap a slice of bacon around each pinwheel, fastening it with a toothpick. Place the pinwheels on a broiler rack, and toast them under moderate broiler heat, turning often until the bacon is cooked. Arrange the pinwheels on a chop plate and serve with stuffed olives.

85

HOT SCRAMBLED EGG CANAPES

2 *eggs, slightly beaten*
3 *tablespoons chopped ham,*
cervelat, salami, or other
sausage
1 *teaspoon minced parsley*

Salt and pepper
Butter or margarine
Toasted bread bases
Grated cheese

Combine eggs with ham or sausage and parsley. Season to taste and cook in butter or margarine over low heat until thick but not dry. Mix with fork while cooking. Spread on toasted bread bases. Sprinkle with cheese. Just before serving, broil under moderate heat until cheese melts. Serve hot.

HOT MUSHROOM CANAPES

1 *cup chopped mushrooms*
2 *tablespoons butter*
½ *cup ground cooked ham*
1 *tablespoon pepper relish*

1 *tablespoon salad dressing*
Bread, sliced thin
Stuffed olives
Pimiento

Sauté mushrooms in butter 5 minutes. Add ham and cook 3 minutes. Stir in pepper relish and salad dressing. Spread on toast rounds. Bake in very hot oven (450° F.) 3 to 5 minutes. Garnish with sliced olives and pimiento strips. Yield: 30 canapés.

CURRIED BUTTON MUSHROOMS

Sauté whole small mushrooms in butter. Season with salt and curry powder. Serve hot on picks.

HOT STUFFED MUSHROOM CANAPES #1

Spread toast rounds with Pimiento Butter. Top with sautéed mushroom cap filled with ground meat or fish mixed with relish and salad dressing. Bake in very hot oven (450° F.) about 5 minutes.

HOT STUFFED MUSHROOM CANAPES #2

12 *large mushrooms*
1 *small onion, minced*
3 *tablespoons butter or*
margarine
¾ *cup minced ham or drained*
spinach purée

Salt and pepper
Salad oil
Grated cheese
Toast rounds

Wash mushrooms quickly. Remove stems. Chop stems and sauté with onion in butter about 3 minutes. Add ham or spinach purée and season to taste with salt and pepper. Dip the whole mushrooms in oil and place in baking dish. Fill with mixture. Sprinkle with grated cheese. Bake in moderate oven (350° F.) about 15 minutes. Serve on toast rounds. Yield: 12 canapés.

HOT STUFFED MUSHROOM CANAPES #3

Use caps of large mushrooms. Sauté and stuff with a mixture of fine buttered breadcrumbs, sautéed minced mushroom stems, minced onion, and seasonings to taste. Sprinkle with grated cheese. Broil until cheese melts. Serve hot on small toasted canapé bases.

SAUTEED ARTICHOKE HEARTS

Drain canned hearts well. Sauté in butter until lightly browned. Sprinkle with salt, pepper, lemon juice, and minced parsley.

ARTICHOKE HEARTS—CRISP FRIED

1 package frozen artichoke hearts   ½ cup flour
1 egg   ½ teaspoon baking powder
½ cup milk   Salt and pepper to taste

Thaw artichokes thoroughly and quarter if so desired. Make batter with egg, milk, flour, baking powder, and add salt and pepper to suit taste. Dip artichokes in batter and fry to golden brown. Serves 4.

Artichoke Hearts—Crisp Fried

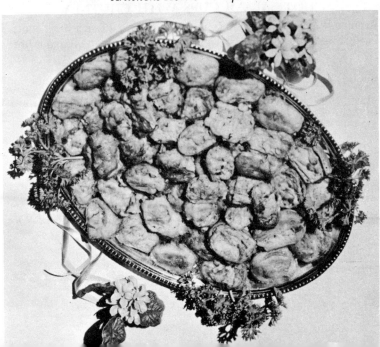

BAKED STUFFED PRUNES

Steam large prunes until tender but firm. Remove pits and fill each with a small pitted or stuffed olive. Wrap each prune in a thin slice of bacon. Arrange on rack in baking pan with end of bacon under prune to hold it in place. Bake in hot oven (400° F.) about 10 minutes or until bacon is crisp. Serve on small squares or rounds of lightly toasted bread.

BROILED STUFFED PRUNES

Steam large prunes until almost tender. Carefully remove pits and stuff cavities with American, Roquefort, or Swiss cheese. Wrap each in small strips of very thin bacon. Secure with picks. Broil under moderate heat until bacon is crisp. Replace burnt picks with clean ones.

HOT WATERMELON PICKLES

Wrap cubes of watermelon pickle in half-cooked strips of bacon. Secure with picks. Bake in moderate oven (350° F.) until hot.

HOT SALAMI AND EGG CANAPES

1 *cup ground, hard salami*
4 *to 6 eggs*

1 *onion, minced*
Salt and pepper

Beat all ingredients together until frothy. Drop by spoonfuls into a well greased hot skillet. Serve on canapé bases spread with mustard.

HOT SALAMI CUPS WITH CHUTNEY

Arrange thin slices of salami on a baking sheet. Place a little chutney in the center of each slice. Broil until edges curl up and filling is hot.

TOASTED PEANUT BUTTER CANAPES

½ *cup peanut butter*
1 *cup milk*
½ *teaspoon salt*

¼ *teaspoon pepper*
1 *egg, slightly beaten*
12 *slices bread*

Cream together peanut butter and milk. Add salt and pepper, then add slightly beaten egg. Remove crusts from bread slices and cut into narrow strips. Dip in the mixture and sauté in butter.

HOT RED PEPPER CANAPES

2 *hard-cooked eggs, minced*
1 *tablespoon canned red*
  pepper, minced
¼ *teaspoon salt*
⅛ *teaspoon dry mustard*

2 *tablespoons grated sharp*
  American cheese
Melted butter
6 *rounds rye bread*

88

Mix together the eggs, red pepper, salt, mustard, cheese, and enough melted butter to make a paste. Fry the bread rounds in deep hot fat (390° F.). Drain and cool. Spread them evenly with the paste and place in an extremely hot oven (500° F.) for 3 minutes. Garnish with watercress and serve hot.

SARDINE-CHEESE CANAPES

Brush oblong toast canapé bases with sardine oil. Top with a sardine. Sprinkle with grated Parmesan cheese. Broil until lightly browned.

BACON-TOMATO CANAPES

Cover rounds of buttered toast with thick slices of tomato. Season tomato slices with salt, paprika, and brown sugar. Cover with small thin bacon strips. Broil until bacon is crisp.

APPETITE TEMPTERS

Small bread rounds   *1 smoky pasteurized process*
Salad dressing   *cheese food link, sliced*
Sliced dill pickles

Spread each round of bread with salad dressing. Cover with a slice of pickle, then with a slice of cheese food. Place under low broiler heat until the cheese food is melted.

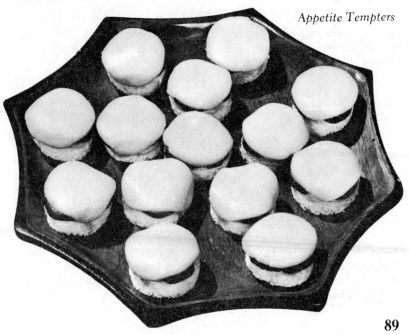

Appetite Tempters

HOT ANCHOVY CANAPES

Arrange flat anchovy fillets on buttered toast strips. Sprinkle liberally with grated Parmesan cheese. Broil under moderate heat until cheese melts.

HOT BOLOGNA ROLLS

Cut thin slices of bologna. Spread with mixture of cream cheese, chopped pickles, chopped chives, and chopped olives. Roll slices and fasten each with toothpicks. Dip in salad dressing seasoned with ketchup and Worcestershire sauce. Broil a few minutes. Serve hot.

HOT BACON-AVOCADO CANAPES

Mash avocado pulp with fork. Season with salt, paprika, and lemon juice to taste. Spread on toast strips. Sprinkle with chopped bacon. Broil until crisp.

HOT PEANUT BUTTER AND BACON CANAPES #1

Mix peanut butter with diced, crisp bacon. Toast rounds or squares of bread on one side. Spread untoasted side with mixture. Place under broiler just long enough to heat slightly.

HOT PEANUT BUTTER AND BACON CANAPES #2

Spread untoasted side of canapé bases with peanut butter. Cover with small thin strips of bacon. Toast in broiler until bacon is crisp.

HOT DEVILED CRACKERS

¼ cup butter	Dash of Worcestershire sauce
2 teaspoons dry mustard	½ teaspoon paprika

Cream butter until soft. Mix thoroughly with other ingredients. Spread on thin crackers. Bake in moderate over (350° F.) until delicately brown.

BRAZIL AND HAM TOASTIES

Trim thin slices of white bread to make 3-inch squares. Spread squares with deviled ham and sprinkle with chopped Brazil nuts. Press nuts into ham. Add, if desired, a slight sprinkling of grated onion. Bring together 2 opposite corners of squares of bread. Fasten with toothpicks to form cornucopias. Brush outside of bread lightly with melted butter. Toast in broiler or hot oven. Serve hot.

Index